W9-CMG-654

Tadeusz Dajczer

THE GIFT OF FAITH

Second Edition
with Foreword by
Theodore Cardinal McCarrick

In the Arms of Mary
FOUNDATION
COMMUNION OF LIFE WITH CHRIST THROUGH MARY

Originally published as *Rozważania o wierze*
Edycja św. Pawła
Częstochowa 1992

English translation previously published in Ireland as *Inquiring Faith*

Imprimatur
Most Rev. Christopher Jones, Bishop of Elphin

In the Arms of Mary Foundation edition 2001
Printed in the United States of America

Published by
In the Arms of Mary Foundation
P.O. Box 271987
Fort Collins, CO 80527-1987
E-mail address: inquiry@IntheArmsofMary.org
Website: www.IntheArmsofMary.org

For more information about the Foundation "In the Arms of Mary" or to obtain additional copies of this book, please visit us at our website.

Scriptural excerpts from the *New Jerusalem Bible* and the
Revised Standard Version Catholic Edition

Cover page design by
Families of Nazareth Movement in U.S.A.

ISBN-10: 0-9721432-0-3 / ISBN-13: 978-09721432-0-2

CONTENTS

Part One

The Virtue of Faith

Part Two

The Dynamism of Faith

Part Three

The Actualisation of Faith

Contents 7

Foreword to the American Edition

 Archdiocese Of Newark
Office of the Archbishop

"The Gift of Faith"

In recent years, our country has been plagued with powerful hurricanes and wildfires of enormous proportions, making many people feel quite powerless. While some are bewildered at the sheer force and destruction caused by these phenomena, others try to make sense out of it, attempting to explain in various ways these forces of nature. Why do they happen? How should we learn from them or interpret them? We search for the answers, even when we can't be totally at peace and secured on our own in this contingent world.

When we look at different aspects of our own life, whether in the area of natural phenomena or politics, sports or social life, we clearly see that it is important to us to grasp the deeper meaning of things – to try to figure out or understand the unpredictable, to bring things to some conclusion. We also want to know and penetrate the mystery of God, to uncover the spiritual meaning of events in all of our happenings. In this way, even as we wrestle and look for the answers from our purely human point of view, we are really constantly searching for the deeper spiritual truth, remembering the words of Jesus Christ "You will know the truth and the truth will set you free." Strangely enough, this quest, or hunger, for the spiritual meaning of various events in our life seems to be stronger and more constantly reoccurring than our concern about the forces of nature and their sudden manifestations in recent years. We yearn for a deeper faith, the kind of faith that withstands the "storms" of life and "gives us the ability to perceive God's will in phenomena and to see events as signs of God's passing by".

This book, **The Gift of Faith,** allows us to draw closer to the more complete reality of our existence and our journey. Through its depth, it can enable us to see our faith through powerful stories, and by shedding meaningful light on the desert experiences of our journey, it teaches that "every moment of your life is a moment of meeting with the Presence that is loving you" (p. 25, bold face). The author of this excellent book focuses on three aspects of faith, each presented in separate parts of this book: *the gift and virtue of faith, deepening of our faith, and our call to live that faith through the example of the Blessed Mother.*

In the first part of this book, the author describes the gift and virtue of faith as God's invitation to participate in His life, to the point of hungering for the ability to entrust ourselves totally to Him. This attitude of self-abandonment to our loving God can be developed in us only to the extent to which we become "Poor in Spirit". Giving us inspiring examples in the saints, such as St. Paul the Apostle, St. Therese of the Child Jesus and St. Maximilian Kolbe, the author shows us what it means to be poor in spirit (p. 58). Realizing that we need some practical tools in overcoming the "seeds of distrust" in us, the author goes on to assure us that "by stirring then within yourself acts of faith, you will in every situation entrust yourself as a child into the arms of the loving Father", while at the same time, echoing the thoughts of "the Little Flower", he sends us a friendly warning: "In the moment that you cease to be a child before the Lord, there will be a crisis in spiritual life and you will regress; you will stop believing and loving" (p. 72). Consequently, only when a Christian can become a child and/or a contrite sinner, can he be truly amazed at the folly of the Father's love, who "so loved the world that He sent His only son".

The second part of **The Gift of Faith** invites us to consider deepening our faith and shows us in what different ways God calls us to rely more on Him. "Faith can become a buried talent if we do not grow in it". That is why

God allows difficult situations to take place which forces us to make choices continually and then truly to grow in Faith. The dynamism of faith becomes reality through trials which polarize human attitudes (p. 75). For example, instead of focusing so much on our faults and imperfections, which leads us to sadness and even sometimes to depression, we should instead desire that God turn every one of our faults into a "felix culpa" – a happy fault (p. 78). We are reminded, especially through the well-known story of the prodigal son, that our true and radical conversion always requires "contrition of heart and longing for forgiveness" (p. 81). I was glad to see that the author dedicated an entire chapter to the timely topic of how to avoid self-preoccupation. The author calls it "a pinch of humor amidst faith". It is reassuring to be reminded that Christian humor "is a remedy by which the idol of your 'self' is dethroned...your vanity and pride become unmasked; that which pretended to be great or to be the threat arousing fear in you is ridiculed and unmasked. In this way, the religious remedy of humor also has the significant role of preserving your psychological balance" (p. 97-98). There is great insight in the author's understanding of the psychology of the spiritual life. We are told, "the gift of the desert forces you to make choices" (p. 127). One takes great consolation in the words "the desert is not only a place where our faith is born, but it ultimately becomes the birthplace and dwelling place of our contemplation" (p. 131), since upon experiencing our weakness (in the desert), we are called by God to throw ourselves into His merciful arms.

In the third and final part of **The Gift of Faith,** we are shown how the Holy Spirit wants to lead us to the faith-filled response evident in loving and serving our Church, following the example of our Blessed Mother. Being both the Mother of the Church as well as "the memory of the Church" (p. 202), Mary espouses the kind of attitude for which we hope, complete abandonment to God with child-like trust and total dedication to service to the Church. It is our Blessed Mother who teaches us how to keep our faith alive and vibrant by daily adherence to the Word of God. Our closeness to Mary assures greater openness to the Holy Spirit. Being open to the Holy Spirit gives us many means of growth in the practice of our faith. The author gives many examples of this.

I would consider this book, **The Gift of Faith,** as a special gift of the Jubilee Year which will help the faithful to experience the renewal of their own faith. **The Gift of Faith** makes us search for the deeper, spiritual meaning of our Life Journey and provides a new building block in the development of a deeper inner spirituality.

Most Reverend Theodore E. McCarrick
Archbishop of Newark

September 25, 2000

Foreword to the Irish Edition
by the Most Rev. Christopher Jones,
Bishop of Elphin

There is very obviously a crisis of Faith in Ireland today. The crisis reveals itself in various ways eg. in the decline of numbers worshipping on Sundays or celebrating the sacraments, in the increase of numbers who are living together outside of marriage, and of children born to single parents together with all the public scandals of State and Church. Our only way back to the living of Gospel values is by rediscovering Faith in our lives.

This Book "Enquiring Faith" by Fr. Tadeusz Dajczer, Professor of the Academy of Catholic Theology, Warsaw comes when it is most needed. I do hope and pray that many, many of our people will have the opportunity of reading it and reflecting seriously on its contents.

Fr. Tadeusz has that special gift of being able to communicate profound theological thoughts in words that are easy to understand.

"The world begins to speak of God, focuses our attention on God, draws us to Him, becomes a sign of His presence, helps us to get in touch with Him and becomes a place where we encounter Him" (*Enquiring Faith*) as soon as we begin to see with the eyes of Faith, hear with the ears of Faith and love with hearts full of Faith. "To live in faith means to be able to see the loving and constantly bestowing presence" of God.

"Every moment of your life is a moment of meeting with the presence that is loving you" (*Enquiring Faith*).

These words from "Enquiring Faith" are the words that set the scene for a splendid treatise on faith. Throughout the entire book the author uses compelling illustrations from the writings of Saints such as St. Theresa of the Child Jesus, St. Francis of Assisi, St. Teresa of Avila, St. Augustine to demonstrate how faith can transform our entire way of looking at life and at all the experiences of life.

"Everything is a gift" (*Enquiring Faith*). The author helps us to see that every experience of life even the experience of failure can be an opportunity of growth in our love for God and for each other if with the gift of faith we can see our world through the eyes of Christ. He quotes from St. Augustine: "For the ones who love God all things work for good, even sin". "You had a lot of trouble today Mother Agnes said to the ailing Theresa". "Yes she answered – but since I love it... I love everything that God gives me" (*Enquiring Faith*).

I read this book during my vacation and thank God for it. The thoughts have helped me to see every experience as a Gift from God and an opportunity to grow in His love. I loved the reflection on Pope John Paul II relating to the attack on his life in October 1981. I quote these words of the Pope from page 138 of "Enquiring Faith";

"While speaking to thousands of pilgrims, he said these significant words:

«God allowed me to experience suffering through the past months, allowed me to experience my life in peril, and allowed me at the same time to understand clearly and profoundly that this is His special grace for myself as a person. It is a grace for the Church as well, since I serve as successor of St. Peter. Christ gave me this grace that I may give testimony of His love through suffering and the danger to my life and health. I find this to be a particular grace and for this I offer special thanksgiving to the Holy Spirit and to the Immaculate-Virgin Mary.»

Without humble means, without the suffering which marks the life of John Paul II, could he have so effectively been the shepherd of the Church"?

Reflection on these beautiful thoughts of Pope John Paul II should help us enormously to accept the bad days with the good days and with the eyes of Faith see all of them as grace-filled opportunities.

CONCLUSION

I thank and congratulate Fr. Tadeusz for this publication. Our world today promotes the pursuit of power, status, wealth and pleasure. The spiritual dimension of life is forgotten. God is pushed more and more from the centre to the sidelines of our hearts, our homes and our communities. The more self-sufficient we get. The less room there seems to be for faith, for God.

Our faith is not in priests, bishops, the Church. Even though they colour it. Our faith is in Jesus Christ who came to open our hearts to the mystery of God the Father. Jesus is proof that God so believes in people that he died for us, in Christ. Jesus is proof that the only God worth searching for is the God who first searched for us when he made his Son like us in all things but sin.

Our personal prayer, our family prayer and our community worship will nourish our faith and help us rediscover that God must really be at the centre of our lives because He must be our first love.

Faith is a way of seeing, not just what is on the surface, but what is beneath it. It is a gift from God, given as a way of finding God in the bits and pieces of our lives. It will help us give praise on the good day. And it will support us on the bad day. It is in the hand of God, leading us through the maze of life.

† Christopher Jones

Foreword to the French Edition
by Rev. René Laurentin

Poland, after her martyrdom and victory over communism, has become a pilot country for the Church – a dwelling-place of creativity. In response to the new needs of our times, especially the most profound and spiritual needs such as prayer and evangelisation, a number of movements and communities have developed: The Apostolic Movements – Family of Families (1952), Auxiliaries of the Mother of the Church (1972), Light and Life (1973); Pro-Life Movements – *Gaudium vitae* (1979), *Pro family* (1982); *Totus Tuus* (1979), Covenant of Families (1981). Elsewhere I have prepared a long list of these recently arisen movements. Among these is *The Families of Nazareth Movement*.

This movement, approved less than 10 years ago has a much longer history. Rev. Tadeusz Dajczer a professor at the Academy of Catholic Theology[1] in Warsaw, being gifted with the charisma of spiritual direction, founded among students a group of explorers of spiritual life. This occurred during the heroic period of the seventies. In 1985, the movement was officially founded with the approbation of Cardinal J.Glemp, Primate of Poland. It numbered over 600[2] members at that time.

Our times are characterised by a great disintegration of the family. This is indicated by Church statistics as well as national statistics. Already during the time between the wars, André Gide proclaimed: 'Families, I hate you!'. The rampant materialism and eroticism, the ideologies of radical feminism and homosexualism (in which an American official of state saw the solution to the problem of overpopulation), as well as legislation, all joined forces in a conspiracy to destroy the foundations of the family. However, Fr. Tadeusz did not wage a war or engage in polemics. The most important thing for him was for the spiritual life to thrive in contact with God Himself. This is what will conquer and neu-

---

[1] Recently transformed into the University of Cardinal Wyszyński.
[2] At present (1999) the number of members in the Movement in Poland amounts to over 20 thousand and in the whole world – a few hundred thousand.

tralise destructive forces. Thus, Fr. Tadeusz contributes to the plan of the Holy Father, whose desire is to support the Church on two complementary and fundamental institutions and strengths: the priesthood and the family.

The Families of Nazareth Movement strives to develop in the family (as the basic cell in the Church and in society) as well as in everybody's life (priests, religious, and celibates) what Jesus Christ wanted: "that they might have life and have it more abundantly" (Jn 10:10). The source is Jesus Christ Himself. The Son of God in order to become man, gave and entrusted Himself completely to His Mother. Now He invites us to entrust ourselves to our Mother. Being involved in the wonderful exchange of the Incarnation where God assumes everything human so that we may share in His life, Mary guards the fulfilment of this plan of God, according to her mission as the Mother of the disciples to whom she was given at the foot of the Cross. Now He invites us to entrust ourselves to our Mother, a Mother who was involved in the wonderful exchange of the Incarnation where God assumes everything human so that we may share in His life. Mary guards the fulfilment of this plan of God according....

This was clearly perfectly understood by John Paul II, who has taken his Marian motto from Louis-Marie Grignion de Montfort: *Totus Tuus* – Totally Yours.

The goal of the Families of Nazareth Movement is sanctity. Jesus wants us to realise the need to enter upon the path to sanctity and to appreciate spiritual direction as being indispensable so as to avoid losing one's way continually, a condition which is so predominant today. This results in a special dynamic of evangelisation.

Various charismas developed in the group led by Fr. Tadeusz and the Movement has spread to 10 countries[3]. It is approved by the Church in Mexico, Columbia, Spain and Portugal. It is also developing in England, Italy, Hungary, Germany and even in France, a country particularly

---

[3] At present the Movement is present in all of the continents.

resistant to deeply spiritual movements which try to implant themselves there.

For example, in June 1989, five Catholics from Mexico touched and drawn by the spirituality of the Movement, came to Warsaw. The movement was founded in Mexico the following year. Presently in Mexico there are 10 thousand members – three times more than in Poland.

The fruitfulness of the Movement is both deep and at the same time discreet; it inspires to evangelisation and gives birth to vocations which brings to mind the maxim: "Noise does not make good. Good does not make noise". No uproar, no publicity. The Movement spreads by word of mouth.

The Movement is founded on *faith*. It is to faith that Fr. Tadeusz devoted his book, published first in Mexico, then in Poland[4]. The book as the Evangelical good seed, yields great harvest.

It guides people along the way of conversion, it is a *call* to sanctity. It is easy to read, although it is demanding. It is directed to everyone, as it flows out of the following evident truth: "We should be completely devoted to God. He gave us everything that we have. We should be ready to give everything back to Him". It is therefore a call for the radicalism in our faith. This book teaches and poses questions. Often the tone of teaching provides a place for dialogue: If someone whom you loved very much lost trust in you, then you know how painful this is. – Would you inflict such pain to the infinite Love of God?

However, this teaching avoids all tactless pressure. Father Tadeusz leads towards the Christian experience of the 'hundredfold', promised by Jesus here on earth to those who

---

[4] The book was then published in France, Spain (in Spanish and Catalan), Italy, Portugal, Columbia, the Philippines, Russia, the Ukraine, Lithuania, Latvia, Bulgaria, Romania, Czech Rep. and Slovakia. It will soon be published in Flemish, German, Chinese, Hungarian, Albanian, Japanese, Arabic, Tagalog as well as in new English versions in the USA, Canada and Australia. It is also being translated into Norwegian, Bielorussian and Croatian.

give everything to Him, and invites us without tactless pressure to do likewise. He shows us the joy of life with God and in Him. Due to this, Fr. Tadeusz refers to the radicalism of faith expressed by the motto in the Gospel: "Whoever finds his life will lose it, and whoever loses his life for my sake will find it" (Mt 10:39).

There is nothing of a warped mystique in this. This is *a call* to sanctity in everyday life. The book invites the reader to develop an awareness of what faith does in us and to contemplate what God in His Love hopes from us. It is based on the theology of spiritual life, greatly influenced by St John of the Cross, St Thérèse of Lisieux and St Maximilian Kolbe. People led by Fr. Tadeusz find his spiritual radiance present throughout this book.

This book is a guide on the path of faith. The author reveals in this book his experiences including that of spiritual direction, to which he has devoted most of his life.

The path to faith is marked by three stages:
1. The Lord invites us to share in His Divine life, and in His love He looks for our coming regardless of our sinfulness.
2. Faith is a dynamic strength, but God reveals His presence, His power, and induces us to be converted through humble means.
3. This dynamism requires strong sustenance: the Eucharist, the Word of God and interior prayer of the heart.

The crucial and simple message of Fr. Tadeusz is a pure source of truth in the context of so many religious deviations widespread today. It is a message consistent with the program of John Paul II, which is enlivened today with a new breath of the Holy Spirit. The author of this profound book does not forget the significance of humour. It is a redemptive exorcism for the deceitful plans of Satan and for the web of vanity which we often fall into.

Paris, September 20th 1992

René LAURENTIN

Document of the Vatican Secretariat of State

original text

SECRÉTAIRERIE D'ÉTAT

———

PREMIÈRE SECTION · AFFAIRES GÉNÉRALES

N. 324.500

DU VATICAN. le 3 avril 1993

Mon Père,

A l'issue de la messe à laquelle vous aviez pris part avec Monsieur Dominique Dupont, dans la chapelle privée, vous avez remis au Saint-Père les <u>Méditations sur la foi</u> du Père Tadeusz Dajczer, fondateur du mouvement des familles de Nazareth.

J'ai le plaisir de vous transmettre les remerciements chaleureux du Pape pour ce geste qu'il a apprécié. L'auteur guide pas à pas son lecteur sur les chemins de la vie spirituelle, avec simplicité et profondeur. Il met en relief le mouvement de la foi et sait montrer comment l'union au Christ est source de vie pour le chrétien. En vous souhaitant de trouver dans cet ouvrage la matière d'un apostolat fécond, le Saint-Père vous accorde de grand coeur, à vous-même et à Monsieur Dupont, sa Bénédiction apostolique.

Veuillez agréer, mon Père, l'expression de mes sentiments tout dévoués.

Sandri

Mgr L. Sandri
Assesseur

Père Jean-Pierre BERNY
SAINT-MICHEL-SUR-ORGE

Document of the Vatican Secretariat of State

– regarding „Enquiring Faith" (French title: „A l'Ecole de la Sainte Famille, Méditations sur la foi"), sent to Fr. Jean Pierre Berny, moderator of the Families of Nazareth Movement in France, after he gave this book to the Holy Father on 31/3/1993.

State Secretariat
Section One – General Affairs
No. 324.500

Vatican City, April 3, 1993

Dear Father,

After the Mass that you took part in with Mr. Dominique Dupont in the private chapel, you gave the Holy Father a book entitled „Méditations sur la Foi" by Fr. Tadeusz Dajczer, the founder of the Families of Nazareth Movement.

It is my pleasure to relay the Pope's sincere thanks to you for this gesture, which he highly appreciates. The author guides the reader step by step on the paths of spiritual life with simplicity and profoundness. He emphasises the development of faith and knows how to portray, that unity with Christ is the source of life for a Christian. The Holy Father extends, with all his heart, his apostolic Blessing to you and to Mr. Dupont, wishing that you find in this work, the means for a fruitful apostleship.

Please accept the expression of my sincere feelings.

Mgr. L. Sandri
Assessor

Rev. Jean-Pierre BERNY
SAINT-MICHEL-SUR-ORGE

Part One

The Virtue of Faith

Faith, what does it mean? The theological virtue of faith is particularly complex. Presented herein, the reality of faith is understood not in terms of dogmatic theology, but in terms of the theology of spiritual life. The faith of the New Testament is man's response to the revelation of God in Jesus Christ. Faith is sharing in the life of God. It is experiencing God's life within us which allows us to see ourselves and the reality surrounding us as if we were seeing it through the eyes of God. It is the adherence to Christ, our Master, our Lord, our Friend. It permits us to rely on Christ, the never failing rock of our salvation, and to entrust ourselves to His infinite power and boundless love. In the face of our human helplessness, faith becomes the continuous resort to the limitless mercy of God and the awaiting of everything from Him (cf. G. Thils, Sainteté chretienne, 359).

Chapter 1

Faith as Sharing in the Life of God

St Thomas Aquinas says that faith brings us closer to God's knowledge of reality. **By sharing in God's life, we start to see and evaluate everything as if through His eyes** – *omnia quasi oculo Dei intuemur* (*In Boeth. de Trinitate*, qu 3, a.1).

Sharing in God's life through faith, causes us to become 'a new person'; we obtain a new comprehension of reality, a new perception of God as well as a new perception of the temporal reality around us. Through faith, we begin to perceive in the temporal reality the actions of the first cause, the works of God. We notice His presence and work within ourselves as well as in the world of nature and history. We notice that He is the author and creator of everything. We realise that what we come to know only in human and worldly terms is not complete reality; it is seeing merely the surface, seeing only the secondary causes which God employs.

Faith is a virtue, which allows us to be in touch with God, and is fundamental to supernatural life. Since faith is fundamental to all supernatural works, everything happens because of it. The positive qualities or short comings of our faith determine the activity of our supernatural life. Difficulties in supernatural life always stem from a weakness of faith. Faith is the basic virtue, since it gives us the possibility of sharing in the life of God. Faith is a sharing in God's thinking. It is as if supernatural reason were placed upon the natural faculties of the soul. Faith allows us to think as God does, not only about ourselves but also about everything we come in contact with. Therefore, to have faith means to synchronise our thought with His thought and to identify ourselves with His thought.

The difference between knowing naturally and knowing through faith is not merely a difference of degree but of the essence of the matter. Faith brings about our unity with God's thinking and an internal sharing in the light in which God knows Himself. In this sense, it leads to contemplation and is an introduction to the future knowledge of God in eternal life.

Since it is through faith we penetrate into the life of God, into the life of Jesus Christ, then it is through this same faith that God begins His own life within us. The purpose of our faith is for us to think as Jesus Christ does; to allow Him, who is living in us through faith, to use us, think within us, and live in us.

Because faith can accomplish in us a complete change from our former way of seeing, thinking, feeling and experiencing, it changes our mentality. It tells us always to place God first, to be concerned about focusing our entire lives on Him, and to interpret the world in the divine light coming from God. Then the light of faith illuminates all of our judgements, appraisals, desires and expectations. In such a way communion of faith is brought about, communion which will realise its fullness only in love.

The created world surrounding us is a voice which speaks to us. If our faith is weak, then that voice will distract us, pull us away from God and focus our attention on itself. As faith grows, the opposite process occurs. The outside world begins to speak of God, focuses our attention on God, to draw us to Him, to become a sign of His presence, to help us get in touch with Him, and to become a place where we encounter Him.

Faith enables us to overcome pretences and to see the primary cause above secondary causes. It allows us to see that all that happens around us does not happen due to man's power. Faith allows us to discover the traces of God in creation. It gives us the ability to perceive God's will in phenomena and to see events as signs of God passing by.

To Perceive the Loving Presence

Every moment of our lives is permeated with the Presence that loves and bestows. To live in faith means to be able to see this loving and constantly bestowing Presence. Because of faith, Christ gradually becomes a light which shines through a person's whole life and which shines through the world. He becomes a living, active Presence in the life of His disciples. Every moment of our lives brings us His presence. Time is the Presence written with a capital 'P'. It is the presence of Christ in our lives. It is the personal presence of God, revealing Himself as the One who expects something from us. God reveals Himself to us through His will.

But what is His will? It is always that which is best for us, because God is Love. *Every moment of your life is a moment of meeting with the Presence, that is loving you.* Someone has said that time is the sacrament of the meeting between man and God. This means that every moment is an evangelical gift, since it is the Presence that calls us to do something. God links grace to each moment, be it an easy or difficult one. St Paul says that we live, move and exist in God (cf. *Ac* 17:28). It is from Him, therefore, that we receive not only the gift of our existence, but also the gifts of breathing, food, friendship and the gift of every moment of our lives.

The statement of St Thérèse of the Child Jesus, that "everything is grace" ("tout est grâce", cf. *Le Carnet Jaune* de Mere Agnes, 5.VI.1897) means that everything that happens in your life, is linked with some kind of grace. God comes to you in the form of a gift, in the form of grace, in the form of a call, in this sense everything is a grace. God wants everything to become for you a 'capital' of good. He even tries to draw good out of evil. Evil cannot be a grace, but God in His almighty and infinite mercy can even draw good from it. The consequences of evil can give fruit in the form of a great opportunity to be converted. Therefore, "everything is a grace" and everything is a 'gift', as always and

everywhere God gives you a chance. It is extremely important for you to believe in this constant Presence which manifests itself in various ways.

The present moment – each moment – brings love, as
Stefan Cardinal Wyszyński has said. Grace is the expression of love, so every moment is linked to God's love, since it
is linked with His grace. Even then, when you commit a
grievous sin, Christ is with you and loves you. If you would
remember this, if you would believe that you are always
immersed in the merciful love of God, who never abandons
you, then it is certain that you would never fall.

*Everything that you experience is linked to the love
of God who loves you, and to His desire for your good.*
He is present in your life no matter what you do. Time is
a sacrament of your meeting with God and His mercy, with
His love for you and with His desire that everything will
work toward your good. Then every fault becomes a 'happy
fault' *(felix culpa).* If you would look in this way during every
moment of your life, then spontaneous prayer would be born
within you. It would be a continuous prayer, since the Lord
is always with you and always loves you. Every moment of
your life, would be permeated with the love of the Presence
that always encompasses you.

Traces of God in the World

Faith allows us to notice the traces of God's works in
everything, to understand that He is present within us, in
our spiritual, emotional and physical lives. *If we know how
to see God in everything, our prayer will become
a prayer of faith,* it will be a prayer not only of words, but
also a prayer of seeing and admiring the world, a prayer of
gratitude for everything which God gives us.

Through faith, we discover that man only appears to be
the protagonist in the history of the world; in reality God is

the main protagonist. The presence of God throughout history affects equally the things that happen in the realm of politics, society and the economy, as well as in our family or in professional matters. He is present everywhere and everything depends on Him. In His hands lay the destinies of all of us as well as the destinies of nations and of the world. We come to know all this through faith, which brings about inner peace in us. This peace flows from faith, which gives us the understanding that He, who is the eternal might and eternal love, holds everything in His hands filled with mercy. He guides everything with His eternal wisdom and total love. Faith gives us the feeling of security and peace, and the confidence that we are *always immersed in God's love*. Faith is a different way of looking at the world, another way of seeing that which is especially difficult. Faith allows us to come to know God in the phenomena of nature, in which we can continually discover the traces of His works and the traces of His concern for us and for the world that surrounds us.

St Francis was a man of great faith who saw traces of God in everything. What incredible faith comes through the attitude of Francis when he prays with the words: "Praise to You, Lord, through brother moon and sister stars. Praise to You, Lord, through brother wind and brother air". Did it ever happen to you while you were walking through a meadow or forest in which the wind blew, that you felt the gentle touch of God in that wind? If so, there is within you something of the faith of St Francis of Assisi, who saw a sign of God's work in everything: "Praise to You, Lord, through brother wind; praise to You who is in this wind. Praise to You for this air that refreshes us, which we can breathe, for You are our breath and our air".

Everything comes from the Lord – good times and the bad. Bad weather is also His weather. Living faith permits us to see God's miracles in the world around us, in our ordinary, everyday lives. Even murky weather and rain are miracles performed for us by God. Rain, which has certainly soaked us more than once, is the Lord's touch. If you see this, this will be your *prayer of faith*.

"Praise to you, Lord, through sister water". By drinking water when we are thirsty, especially on hot and sweltering days, we can experience the presence of the Lord. We are not accustomed to look at the world this way. But in this ordinary, everyday situation we can see God who, through this water, refreshes us and moistens our dry, parched lips. He is in that water. The realisation of this presence is the foundation of faith. That is why St Francis reminds us of 'sister water' – a symbol of God's presence and work.

Talents

God waits for us to look with the eyes of faith at all the experiences we live through, especially the difficult ones. In the parable of the talents, Jesus warns us not to close ourselves off from coming to know Him through faith and not to be slothful in using all things which God is continuously giving us. Upon leaving ten talents to the first servant, five to the second one and one to the third one and obliging them to work, the Master gave them a chance. The word 'talent', which during Christ's times signified a certain monetary value, now signifies an intellectual 'value'. We say that someone is a talented musician or talented mathematician. The meaning of the parable about the talents is however, much more profound. Evangelical thinking is like turning our worldly, purely human thinking inside out. This is also the case in the parable about the talents. A talent is a gift and material, but at the same time an opportunity. *Christ, in giving you a talent, trusts you and waits for you to take proper advantage of it*. If He has given you certain abilities, then He is not indifferent as to what you do with them. And if, however, you did not receive these abilities – this is also a talent. *A talent is not only receiving something, but it is also lacking something*.

In the light of faith, the good health you have is a talent, but bad health is also a talent. Jesus in each case asks the question. What are you doing with this talent? You can equally waste good health, and even more so, you can waste the lack of health. *Everything is a gift; a talent is a gift.* God continuously bestows you with gifts.

It is a talent, for example, if you are unable to pray; yet you consider this as a misfortune. It is important what you do with this inability to pray. Maybe you have buried this talent and you say to yourself: well, I will not pray. But you can gain so much from it. The inability to pray should intensify your hunger for God, and thereby it can become a means contributing to your sanctification.

The same thing applies when you have problems at home, when the family is quarrelling, this also is your talent and an opportunity given to you by God. What can you do with it? If you break down, and are discouraged, then you bury it in the ground. It is not possible for a person of faith not to see the deeper meaning of his own experiences. The very search of the deeper understanding of personal experiences is to profit from the talent. If you experience fear, for example, you fear suffering or death – this is also an opportunity offered to you. St Thérèse of the Child Jesus had a great fear of spiders. Once she told how she had to force herself to remove the spiders' webs from the alcove under the stairs (cf. *The Yellow Notebook*, 13 July 1897, in: *St Thérèse of Lisieux, Her Last Conversations*, p.96). This helped her greatly on her way to the Lord. Placed in her hands was a talent from which she knew how to gain profit.

If certain situations make you feel tense, it means that your talent is hidden within them, as if a diamond were buried beneath the ashes. What do you do with it? How do you make use of it? Everything is meant to serve towards your sanctification. In this sense, everything is grace. Suffering, which overwhelms you or other unfavourable circumstances, is a whole mass of talents. We, however, are often like blind people or like children who understand very little. It is only when we stand before God that everything will be made clear to us. Then we will see the ocean of talents in which we have been immersed.

There are two kinds of talents: those that are less precious and those that are more precious. If you are successful, if something comes out right for you – this is certainly a talent. If however, nothing turns out right – this is a more precious talent. *Failures are the priceless treasures given to you in your life.* Just like the master in the Gospel who returned from his travels and demanded an account from his servants, God will someday ask you, how did you make use of your personal failures, which He gave you as an opportunity, as a talent. Sometimes there are many failures in your life – do you make use of them?

The parable of the talents is an evangelical call to conversion. You have to start looking at your life differently; you must look at it with the eyes of faith. Then you will see God's endless giving of graces; you will see your whole life as a multitude of hidden chances for continual inner transformation. You will come to know that everything is grace. It seems that God, granting you difficult graces, is forcing His gifts into your hands, but you resist and do not want to accept them. *Yet, difficult graces are the most valuable talents of your life.* Sometimes there are many of them because God wants you to have enough talents to make use of.

Faith is sharing in God's vision of reality, but God looks completely differently upon your life. If you have faith, it is like seeing every day of your life, through the eyes of Jesus. Only then will you see the unceasing opportunities for your conversion and sanctification. Then you will also begin to understand suffering, which in the light of faith, is a cross. It is, therefore, something that will transform you spiritually, if you accept it. If, in your difficulties, you recognise the cross as an opportunity toward transformation, then your difficulties truly become gifts for you. If you saw all the countless talents which God is continuously giving you, you would never be sad. Then talents, such as poor health or situations filled with conflicts and failures, would bring joy to your heart, a joy that God bestows on you something invaluable and shows for you an exceptional trust. He trusts that you will not bury or reject His gifts. *He counts on your faith*, since it is only in the light of faith that you can recognise the talents given to you. A talent is everything that you have understood and remembered up to this moment. However, poor memory and the fact that you forget many things is also a talent, because everything brings grace and – in this meaning – everything is a grace.

Only a person who has faith is able to be grateful for everything. This gratitude will be visible on your face as joy; for everything may be changed into good. This reflection about talents refers to the teaching of St Paul and to the famous thesis of St Augustine: "For the ones who love God, all things work for good, even sin" (*Rom* 8:28). Therefore, even a fall, which is a great misfortune, and at the same time hurts Jesus, can be an opportunity within which is hidden some kind of talent given to you in that situation, from which you can profit. You only need your faith or your conversion towards such faith which will enable you to look through the eyes of Jesus. He, looking at your life, that may be filled with failures, problems, conflicts, unfulfilled plans, everyday difficulties and spiritual difficulties, is never sad. He is joyful, because He expects all those things to bear fruit and that you will take advantage of them and you will be joyful and grateful for everything He gives you: "You had a lot of trouble today", Mother Agnes said to the ailing Thérèse of the Child Jesus. "Yes", she answered: "but since I love it... I love everything that God gives me" (cf. *The Yellow Notebook*, 14 August 1897, ibid. p.148).

St Bernadette looked at her life in a similar way. Her 'Testament' is an exceptionally expressive statement of gratitude for the gifts which she received:

For the poverty in which my mother and father lived, for the failure of the mill, for all the hard times, for the awful sheep, for constant tiredness, thank you, my God!

For lips, which I was feeding too much, for the dirty noses of the children, for the guarded sheep, I thank you!

Thank you, my God, for the prosecutor and the police commissioner, for the policemen, and for the harsh words of Father Peyramale!

For the days in which you came, Mary; for the ones in which you did not come, I will never be able to thank you – only in Paradise. For the slap in the face, for the ridicule, the insults, and for those who thought I was mad, those who suspected me of lying, for those who suspected me for wanting to gain something from it, thank you, my Lady.

For my spelling, which I never learned, for the memory which I never had, for my ignorance and for my stupidity, thank you.

For the fact that my mother died so far away, for the pain I felt when my father instead of hugging his little Bernadette, called me "Sister Marie-Bernard", I thank you, Jesus.

I thank you for the heart you gave me, so delicate and sensitive, which you filled with bitterness.

For the fact that Mother Josephine proclaimed that I was good for nothing, thank You. For the sarcasm of the Mother Superior: her harsh voice, her injustices, her irony, and for the bread of humiliation, thank you.

Thank you, that I was the privileged one when it came to being reprimanded, so that my sisters said: "How lucky it is not to be Bernadette".

Thank you for the fact that it is me, who was the Bernadette threatened with imprisonment because she had seen you, Holy Virgin; regarded by people as a rare animal; that Bernadette so wretched, that upon seeing her, it was said: "Is that it?"

For this miserable body which You gave me, for this burning and suffocating illness, for my decaying tissues, for my de-calcified bones, for my sweats, for my fever, for my dull and for my acute pains, thank you my God.

And for this soul which You have given me, for the desert of inner dryness, for Your night and Your lightening, for Your silences and Your thunders, for everything. For You – when You were present and when you were not – thank you, Jesus" (according to *Fonti vive,* Caravate, September 1960).

Chapter 2

Faith as Adhering to Christ

Faith in the subjective sense, is not only sharing in God's life, but is also an existential adherence to Christ as the one Lord and one Love. This implies that each person makes a choice, and steers his will toward Christ as the final goal and greatest priority.

Adherence to Christ is our answer to His call and to His looking upon us with complete love. This answer will always be marked with adventure and also with risk. Jesus wants us to attach ourselves to Him without questioning details, without considering the consequences of our choice and without questioning the future. He wants us to answer "yes" as Mary did; expressing in this way our complete abandonment to God. The essence of trustful abandonment to Jesus and of adherence to Him lies in our accepting the unknown that remains in darkness, and therefore demands faith. Adherence to Christ is the beginning of love. It will be accomplished by the merging of our will with the will of Christ. This is the beginning of our personal communion with God.

Our adherence to Christ is not possible without detaching ourselves from that which can enslave us. The Apostles, in order to follow Christ, had to leave everything. To choose Christ as the supreme value is also to consent that He, Himself, will form us.

"No One Can Serve Two Masters"

Faith, which is the adherence to Christ as the only Lord and our only love, requires turning to Him as to the One who is of greatest value. Total adherence to Christ requires a free heart, therefore a turning away from slavery to 'mammon'. The Gospel says, "No one can serve two masters; for either he will hate the one and love the other, or he will be devoted to one and despise the other. You cannot serve God and mammon" (*Mt* 6:24). There are two masters God and mammon; there is no third one. This is what the highest authority, Jesus Christ, says. The relationship of one master to the other is a relationship of radical contradiction. The Gospel clearly states, "for either he will hate the one and love the other". If you love one master, you hate the other. And further: "be devoted to one and despise the other". If you are devoted to one, then you must despise the other. This is a very strong statement. We cannot, therefore, attach ourselves to Christ and serve Him, while at the same time serve mammon, although we are always exposed to the temptation to compromise and combine that which cannot be combined.

"No one can serve two masters". Who are these 'masters' (*kyrios* in the Greek text)? One is Christ, our one true Lord – *Kyrios*. The other is mammon – the false *kyrios*, the false lord. To serve mammon is to enslave oneself and become dependent on some kind of material or spiritual good. Notice that mammon is called a master, who is served as one serves a king. *We serve God and love Him; hence we despise mammon, that is, we despise our attachment to material or spiritual goods, or* it is terrifying even to think, **we love our attachment to these goods, and as a result we begin,** possibly unconsciously, **to despise God.**

If you analyse your prayer, this will help you to identify what forms and images mammon takes on in your life. *If you take stock of what you are thinking about most often during prayer, then you will see what is your greatest treasure.* "For where your treasure is, there will your heart be also" (*Mt* 6:21). Your distractions will allow you to discover how many attachments to mammon you have. If there are many, do not be surprised that it is difficult for you to concentrate during the rosary, during adoration or during the Eucharist.

The word *kyrios* in the Greek language means absolute ruler and master. On the other hand, the word *douleuein* (to serve) means enslaved servitude to the absolute master and complete ownership by him. The Gospel says that we belong entirely to the Lord, regardless of whether we acknowledge this or not. We are and will always remain the property of the Lord, who is Jesus.

Originally, the Hebrew term 'mammon' meant some kind of treasure, that is, money or expensive things put into a deposit. At that time, it did not have a negative meaning. In the course of time, however, there came about an evolution in the understanding of this term. It started to mean that when you placed expensive things with your banker or someone you trusted, you could then count on your treasure and place your hope in it. This was the first stage of the evolution. Mammon became an object of trust. Then the word 'mammon' started to be written with a capital letter, and at that time it denoted a false lord and master. Then an unusual alienation occurred, *a thing took possession of a person.* Everything in which he placed his hope started to become a god for him.

And you, in whom or in what do you place your hope? What do you count on? Who is your God? If you place your hope in a false god, then you will know bitterness and disappointment, because it is a master that sooner or later will disappoint you. This will be a great grace for you, because then your trust in mammon will begin to crumble.

What can this mammon be, that enslaves your heart? It can be material as well as spiritual goods. For example, it can be attachment to money, to your children, to your work, to something you are creating or working on at present. It may be attachment to peace, or even to one's own perfection. All these attachments cause your bondage and bring you slavery. As a human being you can choose to attach yourself to the one and only reality, that is the will of God. Everything that enslaves you closes you off from God and diminishes your faith.

How can you uncover your mammon? Are tension, stress, restlessness, rushing and sadness that accompany you through life, signs that you serve some kind of mammon? There are people, for example, that live under constant stress. How great then, must be their attachment to something opposed to God? People free from attachments are filled with the peace of God. The peace of God builds and strengthens mental health which in turn reflects on physical health. In this way, the soul, the psyche and the body participate in a person's great freedom. A person free from attachments is also free from facial wrinkles, from stress and from diseases of civilisation. *Mammon systematically destroys a human person.* It not only blocks your way to Christ and your adhering to Him, but it also destroys your health and your psyche.

An obvious *sign of attachments* is also your *sadness in situations when God takes something away from you.* He will therefore, take that which you are enslaved to, hence everything that is your greatest enemy, that which causes your heart not to be free for Him. It is only then, when you start to accept cheerfully these kinds of situations and submit with serenity that you will become more and more free.

During prayer while standing before the Lord, show Him not only your empty hands but also your dirty hands defiled by your attachments to mammon, and pray that He will have mercy on you. Prayer can develop only in the atmosphere of freedom. As a disciple of Christ, you are called especially to contemplative prayer. *For your prayer to become contemplation,* that is, a loving gaze on Jesus Christ, your beloved, *it is essential to have a free heart.* That is why Christ fights so much for your heart to be free. He fights through various events, through difficulties and storms, all the while giving you the chance to co-operate intensely with grace. In all these situations, Christ expects that you will try to cleanse your heart, soiled by attachments and servitude to mammon. Hence, all these difficult moments and all the storms are graces for you. They are the passing by of the Merciful Lord, who loves you so much that He wants to give you this magnificent gift, *the gift of total freedom of your heart.* Your heart should not be divided: it should be a heart solely for Him.

To have faith means to see and understand the meaning of your life in accordance with the Gospel and that God is most important. Your life is to be orientated toward Him, to seek and build primarily His kingdom with faith that everything else will be given to you (cf. *Mt* 6:33). God wants to bestow each person with all His love. However, He can bestow this on a person only to the extent of his openness, and his readiness to be stripped of his attachments, so that room may be made for Him. It is faith that creates in us this emptiness and vacuum in which God can dwell.

The Will of God and Our Own Will

Whether our faith will deepen someday to the point of total adherence to Christ, will depend on our desire to do His will in everything, together with our consent to crucify our own will. To adhere to Christ means to surrender our will to His will. Spiritual life is brought about under continuous tension between the will of God and the will of a person. The tension comes from the fact that we are continuously revolving around our will, around that which is convenient to us, while it is obvious that the scope of our plans and desires, the scope of that which we want, does not correspond to what God wants.

Man is defensive against anything that would be contrary to his own desires. He then is either consciously defensive, when he refuses to submit to the will of God, or there is a similar process happening in his subconscious, which often takes the form of a defence mechanism of his rationalisation. This mechanism shows how much self seeking there is in our desires and efforts.

What is this defence mechanism of rationalisation? It is the subconscious that prescribes motives acceptable to us for our own activities, while at the same time it rejects the true motives not accepted by us. Using everyday language, we could say that in our striving to achieve our hidden desires and intentions, we invent certain self-justifying theories which comfort us. A classic example that illustrates this defence system is a mother defending her son in front of her daughter-in-law.

When the defence mechanism of rationalisation is triggered, the mother will be completely convinced that she is acting out of love only, and that she has that right, since she is his mother and wants only what is best for him. Then, possessive love for her son, which usually occurs in such a case, remains hidden behind the subconscious defence mechanism and the invented subjective theory which justifies such an attitude. When the mother behaves this way it is almost impossible to convince her that she loves only herself through her son, that she is breaking up the marriage, and that she should step aside, or even take the side of her daughter-in-law instead of supporting her son.

The defence mechanism of rationalisation is a fortress so strong and difficult to disarm primarily because it is in the subconscious. How often do we, every one of us, invent some theory to justify our improper behaviour? We say: "After all I must rest, I cannot take care of that; after all I have a right to that; after all I was hurt, I have to defend myself," etc. *You can even be very devoted to a so-called love, to the apostolate, to honourable causes, but at the source of this may lie a hidden and subconscious egoism.*

It is egoism that causes our spiritual life to keep on going in constant tension between our will and the will of God. If living by faith means adherence to Christ and to His will, then in this context it should be emphasised that seeking our own will is the worst thing we could do. It is the source of evil and sin, the source of our misfortune and enslavement. Adherence to Christ and to His will, means that when His will is not in accordance with our will, we accept His ruining our plans. We accept His foiling them. The events in the lives of the saints often show us how God foiled human plans so that the human will could unite with the will of God.

St Teresa of Avila was travelling to Seville, where she intended to found a new monastery. These were difficult times for the reform. Teresa was at that time founding a newly reformed branch of the Carmelite Sisters. The foundation of the convent in a new city required that she go there as the Superior with a group of sisters. The sisters usually travelled in well-covered wagons, because the reformed Carmelite sisters, known as discalced, were cloistered nuns who could not appear in public. Hidden in the covered wagons, they felt safe and hoped that they would arrive at their destination without being seen by anyone because they did not want to cause a sensation by showing themselves.

It was Pentecost Sunday. The sisters departed very early in the morning. Teresa chose a church in the far suburbs of Cordoba, where they had decided to stop. The priest there, Fr. Julián of Avila, was to celebrate Mass for them so that they would not be seen, and the sisters intended later to continue their journey. Soon it became apparent that in order to get to their chosen church, they had to cross a bridge. The bridge at that early hour was closed. The sisters learned that the key could only be issued by a principal official. However, the official was still asleep and had left orders that he must not to be disturbed by such matters. Thus, they had to wait. In the meantime, the sun was rising and it was getting hot. People were starting to gather around the wagons. Some, seeking sensation, even tried to peek into the wagons. Finally after two hours of waiting, the key was brought and the gate was opened. The wagons moved forward, but they proved to be too wide to pass through the gate of the bridge.

More hours passed. St Teresa wanted so much to celebrate the Feast of the Pentecost at an earlier Mass, and it was very important to her that the sisters pass unnoticed. When they finally sawed off the parts of the wagons that were sticking out, and the sisters arrived at the church outside of town, they were met with yet another surprise. It turned out that the church was dedicated to the Holy Spirit, and as always on the Feast of Pentecost there were crowds of people inside and outside the church. This was too much. St Teresa even said that she was ready to forego Mass. The rest of the sisters also were ready to give it up. It was not until later that St Teresa admitted that this could have been a serious mistake. Luckily, Fr. Julián directed the sisters to attend Mass despite the crowds. They came out of the security of their hiding and started to pass through the crowded church. St Teresa who usually had a picturesque manner of speaking said later that when the people saw them under their veils in their white clothes and coarse woollen mantlet, they reacted similar to onlookers at a bullfight when a bull comes into the arena. Teresa said this was one of the really bad moments of her life. This, very bad moment in her life, was granted to her by the Holy Spirit on His feast day.

This was not the end of the difficulties. After Mass, the sisters had to pass once again through the screaming and clamouring crowd, and after coming out, they discovered that because of the intense heat they could not travel further. The horses refused to pull the wagons. Inside the wagons it was so hot and stifling, that the sisters took their siesta under a bridge. None of their plans worked out. (Cf. *The Book of Her Foundations*, Ch.24, 12-14, in: *The Collected Works of St Teresa of Avila*, Vol.3, Washington, D.C. 1985, pg.226-227).

The Holy Spirit can descend upon a person with graces that will ruin all his plans. These are his great graces of detachment. His treatment of Teresa in this manner on the day of Pentecost, showed His great love for her. She had planned and set up everything so perfectly for herself, and He foiled her plans so perfectly because they were not according to His will. In all this, the most important thing was that, **the Holy Spirit 'descended' on Teresa and the remaining sisters, for they accepted his works; surrendering to the will of God, they adhered closer to Christ.** The Holy Spirit, the great Builder of our faith, stripped them and reduced them to poverty so that they could accept the strength of Him, who in the liturgy of the Church is called "The Father of the Poor".

Faith as Relying on Christ and Entrusting Ourselves to Him

Faith is participation in the life of God; it is attachment to Him as the only Lord, as well as our sole reliance on Him. Relying on Christ and totally abandoning ourselves to Him expresses our complete confidence in Him. A person is made to seek out the feeling of security, to seek something to rely on which means he is directed towards self-entrustment to God. He is directed toward having a system of security, towards counting on something, and entrusting himself to something or someone. The feeling of security is the basic, most elementary need of the human psyche. Lack of security creates fear whether in a threatening situation or in a situation when something we rely on is taken away. This fear which arises in us causes us to intensify our efforts to feel secure.

In a material sense we can refer to relying on something and feeling secure, when we count on our possessions, for example, money, talents and abilities. We can also reinforce our feeling of security in a personal sense when we count on contacts and interpersonal relationships aimed towards the realisation of our plans. Often feeling secure in the material sense, is connected with our being orientated toward the future. A person with a strong retention of impressions tries to foresee in detail what will happen in the future and tries to prepare for everything, so that he is not taken by surprise. In this way it is as if he wants to control the future, and seeks in this, something to rely on and a feeling of security.

This kind of search for security is always present in our lives. A student taking an exam bases his security on memory of what he has learned or on his abilities. He can also count on what is called 'luck', but he will try always to rely on something, whether it is in the material or personal sense. Nevertheless, all human systems of security cannot be perfect, since they are based solely on our plans or calculations; that is why they have to fail and then there comes a crisis. If you trust in yourself, in your abilities, in your possessions, or in people that you are connected with, sooner or later you will have to be disappointed.

For our faith to be reliance on Christ and entrustment of ourselves to Him, we have to accept Him as our only true security. Flowing from faith in Christ's Word, complete abandonment to Him is the only adequate response to His unfathomable love for us.

God – the Only One to Rely on

Faith is relying on nothing apart from God. We cannot rely on any of His gifts,only on Him alone, on His infinite power and infinite love.

A moving scene took place in the courtyard of the temple, when it was God who watched people put their donations into the money box. Every few moments the clink of falling coins could be heard, while somewhere on the side, Jesus Christ and his Apostles are sitting and observing those offerings.

A widow puts into the box two small coins worth a penny, and the Lord says: "She put in the most [...] she contributed all she had" (*Mk* 12:43-44). We can admire her deed: she gave all, while the rich gave only from their surplus wealth. Yet, to see just her gesture is not enough. It needs to be pointed out that by giving everything, she 'sentenced' herself to death, since she did not have any more money and no longer had the means to live. She, herself, severed her material system of security. Hence the amazement of God Himself as expressed through the solemn words: "Amen, I say to you [...] she, from her poverty, has contributed all she had, her whole livelihood". Inconceivable is the faith of this woman!

A person who is stripped of everything, his whole system of security, is left with two options: he may either despair, or through faith, completely entrust himself to God. That is the kind of faith the widow must have had. For her, God must have been everything – her only support. God can strip us of our systems of security, but we can also do this ourselves. Then an active purgation of ourselves from enslavement takes place. This is what happened to the evangelical widow, she stripped herself of everything she had.

We can also talk about a similar self-entrusting to God of the widow from Zarephath, who met with Elijah. (cf. *1K* 17:8-16). The widow had a small child and in her country there was a famine. The only things left in her supplies were a handful of flour and a few drops of oil. It is under these conditions that Elijah says to her, "Make me a little cake". The comment of the widow, that these are the last handfuls of flour, changes nothing. Elijah repeats his request, "Make it for me". The woman replies, "Yes, I will do as you ask and then we will starve to death – my child and I". This was really an acceptance of death, since there was nothing left to count on, not even this handful of food. This was God, through Elijah, who took from the widow the remaining food, which had given her a certain feeling of security. Then she had nothing.

What does God do with such people? The Bible says that afterwards the flour increased, so that despite preparing meals, there was always enough. And it was the same with the oil – the widow and her child did not die. God cannot abandon a person, who by totally entrusting himself to Him, frees himself from mammon and cuts himself off from the systems of security that destroy his faith. *God watches with admiration the miracle of human faith, especially trusting, childlike faith, which expresses itself in the act of giving up everything.* A person with such faith is capable of saying, "My: God, if this is Your will, I am even ready to die, since I believe that You love me. *Faith this deep begets saints.*

When Mother Teresa of Calcutta, left her convent of the Indian sisters of the Loreto Order to care for the dying at the temple of the goddess Kali, she obviously had few possessions and little money. However, very quickly, she gives all that she has to the dying. What then?

When night comes, there remains only one thing: "God, if you wish, then I will die". In India, in Calcutta, no one would help her, since people there look with indifference upon dying people. In the context of the Hindu religion and the law of Karma, this state of affairs is considered almost normal. A person of Hindu faith would say to you that since you are dying of starvation, it means that you deserve it. If you die from starvation, you will later be reborn into a better existence after death.

Mother Teresa of Calcutta understood that she might not find anyone willing to help her. At the same time, however, she believed that God was by her side and that from then on she would rely only on Him. There were days and nights, when after giving away everything, Mother Teresa fell asleep in horrible exhaustion. She slept with the certainty that she had nothing for tomorrow; nothing for herself or for the few postulants in the new order and nothing for the mass of dying people who had to be helped.

These were lessons of faith and lessons of holiness for Mother Teresa of Calcutta. She had nothing. In these conditions, in the absence of any human systems of security, Mother Teresa of Calcutta emerges as the one whom the world looks upon with honour and respect. She is a person who has faith, who believes to the point of folly, who went through difficult lessons in gaining faith in situations where humanly speaking there was nothing to rely on.

When our whole system of security falls apart, there remains only despair or faith, either terrible despair or heroic faith.

If your faith is not radical enough and if you do not trust completely God's love for you to the point of folly, then you will continue to advance on your way to faith at a snail's pace or you will go backwards. By building a human system of security, you will hinder your growth in faith. Your faith will deepen only when you allow God to be your only support and your only security. *God has the right to request that you give Him everything, everything in the sense of total self-entrusting to Him.*

From the point of view of faith, it is a very good thing that sometimes our support crumbles beneath us, because grace is linked to this. You cannot rely on anything but God, or on any of His gifts, or on any signs of His presence.

The Old Testament relates to us that after a terrible defeat of the Israelites by the Philistines, which took place during the time of Judges, the Ark of the Covenant got into the hands of the enemy. In the first book of Samuel we read that the Philistines "drew up in line against Israel. After a fierce struggle Israel was defeated by the Philistines, who slew about four thousand men on the battlefield. When the troops retired to the camp, the elders of Israel said, 'Why has the Lord permitted us to be defeated today by the Philistines? Let us fetch the ark of the Lord from Shiloh that it may go into battle among us and save us from the grasp of our enemies'. So the people sent to Shiloh and brought from there the ark of the Lord of hosts, who is enthroned upon cherubim. The two sons of Eli, Hophni and Phinehas, were with the ark of God.

When the ark of the Lord arrived into the camp, all Israel shouted so loudly that the earth resounded. The Philistines, hearing the noise of shouting, said, "Woe to us!" (*1 Sm* 4:2-8). – And the epilogue to this occurrence is: "The Philistines fought and Israel was defeated; every man fled to his own tent. It was a disastrous defeat, in which Israel lost thirty thousand foot soldiers. The ark of God was captured, and Eli's two sons, Hophni and Phinehas, were among the dead" (*1 Sm* 4:10-11).

One may ask, why the Israelites suffered such a great defeat. The Ark of the Covenant was a sign of God's presence among them. Therefore, by asking for it to be brought and by placing in it their hopes for victory, they wanted to rely on Him. How should this be understood, that the Israelites, even though they strove to rely on God, suffered such a defeat and that the Ark – the principal sign of God's presence – was taken from them?

This text is very important, since it allows us a to form a deeper understanding of what it means to rely exclusively on God; the Ark of the Covenant is not God, it is only a sign of His presence. The Israelites had tried to manipulate this principal sign of God for their personal use. The epoch of Judges is a rather depressing time in the history of the Chosen People. We know that in the lives of the Israelites, a lot of evil things were happening, as well as in the lives of the High Priest Eli's sons, who "cared nothing for Yahweh" (*1 Sm* 2:12). In this context the Biblical text shows us how the Israelites, not having respect for the Lord, manipulated the sign of God's presence. They felt that after bringing out the Ark of the Covenant, victory should take place almost automatically. Faith, however, does not rely on any of God's gifts or any signs of His presence, but only on Him alone, on His power and love. This power and love cannot be manipulated.

A similar thing happened with the temple, which was also for the Chosen People a principal sign of God's presence. It was destroyed because it was not meant to be a permanent support for the Chosen People. God called this nation to rely, through faith, solely on Him.

The Attitude of Entrusting Ourselves to God

Christ, who expects us to entrust ourselves to Him, teaches us with His whole life the attitude of total self-entrusting to Him. He came to us as a Child, an Infant, who on its own can do absolutely nothing and is totally dependent on the care of adults. Jesus, therefore, from the moment of coming into this world appears before us stripped of everything. Why did He choose such nakedness? Try to answer this question for yourself.

If Christ had come on earth with His might, if He had annihilated the Roman occupation by force and forced justice upon society, if He had eliminated evil by force, would it have been easier for you to entrust yourself to Him? – It is more likely that you would have been afraid of Him, for man is afraid of violence, even when used in the name of good, real or alleged. You cannot fear the defenceless Jesus who comes to us in His powerlessness. If you fear God, the mystery of Bethlehem reminds you that *you must not fear God*. He humbled Himself so much, stripped himself of everything, and became so defenceless, to make it easier for you to adhere to Him and entrust yourself to Him. In this way, He showed His love, which extends to the point of folly. Christ, stripped of everything and poor, wants us to follow Him on the way to our denudation of human securities. Our true and authentic denudation is our way to imitate Jesus.

God, in wanting to make Abraham the father of our faith, had to uproot him. Abraham became a pilgrim, moving about as if in darkness, since he did not know where he was going. Leaving his own country and home, he became a naked person, a kind of person who, besides God, has nothing. He therefore permanently depended on God and turned to Him. Freedom from one's own system of security can be attained in a desert, which strips one of everything.

The various human systems of security on which you rely, become, in the evangelical definition, mammon. You may believe in it and place all your hopes here, but it is not the real God. *God wants to protect you from false faith in your life*. That is why it is so important to Him that you reject your false god. Everything we place our hope in becomes a god. If you place your hope in a false god, then your hope does not make sense. Whoever has a false god, lacks faith or his faith is very weak and paltry. If, in your life there is a false god whom you serve and on whom you depend then, from necessity, you will come to know bitterness and disappointment. That false master, to whom you have entrusted yourself, in whom you placed your hopes, sooner or later must let you down. Moreover, something in your entrustment to that false master will collapse.

Christ, when saying that you cannot serve two masters, elaborates His thoughts in forms of symbolic images and through them teaches how we should trust – how we should attain that complete entrustment to Him as the true Master. In His Sermon on the Mount, He speaks of the lilies of the field. These flowers are red poppies, the kind that remind us of the poppies of Monte Casino in Italy. Palestinian poppies and anemones are lilies of the field. What is peculiar to them apart from their astonishing beauty is that they are short-lived. This type of flower lives only one day. It is amazing that God creates such a magnificent one-day flower which, as Jesus said, is more magnificent than the greatest splendour of Solomon. How God must care for it, emphasising all the splendour of beauty in it! This flower belongs to the Lord, just as you do.

Speaking about the carefree birds, Jesus appeals to us to be converted and to free ourselves from human tensions, unnecessary worrying, and excessive anxiety (cf. *Mt* 6:26-34). *We are to be like the lilies of the field and like the birds in the sky, which He, the true Lord Himself, loves and cares for.*

The plea in Our Lord's Prayer: "Give us this day our daily bread" is a call to deepen our faith, that God may become our only support. We find here a clear allusion to the situation that occurred in the desert during the exodus of the Chosen People to the Promised Land. Obviously, the desert creates difficult conditions. That is why there were revolts and there was disobedience. The Lord, however, was ignited with a jealous love, as the Bible states, and took pity on his complaining, sinful people, sending them manna which fell to earth each day. Being in the desert brings forth that which is deeply embedded in man; egoism, mistrust, and the desire to create one's own system of security. Among the Chosen People there appeared a lack of trust in God, despite the miracles that were happening. Their greed also surfaced, expressing itself in the need to gather as much manna as possible, even though Moses, in the name of the Lord, warned them: "You may gather enough manna for *today only*". Many, however, did not obey Moses and gathered more.

Then, the next stage of the miracle took place, but in another dimension. The following day all the excess, the amount greater than that which should have been gathered and meant to be the system of security, turned rotten and was eaten by maggots (cf. *Ex* 16:14-21). The Chosen People could not make themselves secure in a human way by accumulating reserves. This was due to the fact that God led them into the desert to strip them of their securities: "Give us this day our daily bread". Give us *this day*, for today, not for tomorrow or for the whole month. We belong to You. You care about that which belongs to You. In the desert, the Lord had to fight with human egoism which caused the Chosen People to refuse to trust in Him in spite of the miracle. He had to fight for the faith of His people.

Maturity in faith means the willingness to give up to the Lord everything that He gives us, entrusting ourselves totally to Him. We should not attach ourselves to anything; not even to spiritual gifts, and not even to Holy Communion. God's will is the only one reality which one may attach oneself to, without claiming it for oneself. Everything besides God's will is a gift and a means to reach the aim, but it is not the aim. If we claim the gift for ourselves, God will either destroy it or – through giving us the experience of suffering – show us that we have nothing to offer, that we are helpless and that it is God who gives us everything.

A truly expressive testimony of St Leopold Mandič's faith was his gesture of showing empty hands. These empty hands turned towards God symbolise his expropriation of any gifts; an expression of extraordinary faith. This faith enabled God to perform miracles through him in the confessional. Our gesture of showing empty hands can be directed towards God not only in spiritual matters as in the case of St Leopold Mandič. It can indicate our attitude of awaiting everything from God, and should accompany us in everything we do in life: in work, in raising our children, in our influence on others and in prayer. The gesture of empty hands should also accompany us when looking for the greatest of God's gifts to come – a gift of He Himself for He is Love, which embraces us and in which we are immersed.

Abandonment to God

Your reliance on God by entrusting yourself to Him will not be completely pure unless it takes on the form of *abandoning yourself to Him.* It could be that you will entrust yourself to Him, expecting that He will fulfil your will. If you say, "God, I entrust myself to you, my will be done", – this is still the constant seeking of oneself. Reliance on God has to become the abandoning of oneself to Him. *Lord let it be as you want,* since You love me and know best what I need, and what those whom I love need, and what those whom I pray for need. In our spiritual life, and on our way to God; our entrusting of ourselves to Him must become a way of total abandonment to the Lord.

At Christmas in 1887, Celine, the sister of St Thérèse of the Child Jesus, wanted to give her a joyful surprise. She made a little paper boat and set it on the water. Inside the boat was a small figurine of a sleeping Jesus and the word: 'Abandonment' (cf. *Manuscrits autobiographiques de Sainte Thérèse de l'Enfant-Jésus,* 1957 p.169-170). This was the catchword of Thérèse's and Celine's prayer. There are waters, the waves of life, on which God will lead them, and they are to abandon themselves to His love.

The theology of spiritual life says that only the abandonment of oneself to God begets internal peace within a person. You will continue to be uneasy, your heart will continue to be as restless as a moth beating against a light bulb. You will be filled with distress, cares and troubles as long as you do not try to abandon yourself to the Lord. *There is no other way to peace than to abandon yourself completely to His will, to His love.*

To St Gertrude, who was praying for the health of her friend, Christ said: "You interfere, Gertrude, asking for her health, since this illness is a great grace, and she is surrendering to My will and is quickly being sanctified". The French word *abandon,* written by Celine for Thérèse on the little boat has very profound meaning. It means renouncing one's own plans and visions, *leaving everything behind so that one can devote oneself totally to the Lord*. We are so full of our own plans and our own visions while God's will and God's plans are often different. Then God must foil our plans. *This foiling of our plans is blessed, for it is His love* which always wants what is best for us.

A big obstacle which can prevent our abandonment to God could be a *distorted image of God*. This distorted image may be that you see God as a Judge, and you are afraid of Him. To fear God, to fear Him who is love, is terrible. Maybe you are afraid to abandon yourself to Him because you are afraid of what He may do with you. You must remember, however, that this kind of *conscious fear of God hurts His Heart deeply*. It is not so with the fear that is instinctive, that arises by itself spontaneously on a psychophysical level, which is really not under your control. If, however, on a spiritual level (in your thoughts and in your will) you consciously consent to fearing God, this is a great unfaithfulness. If you fear God, people, or the world in this way, there is no trust in you, nor do you believe in God's embracing love for you.

St Therese of Lisieux briefly said that one has to be like a child and worry about nothing (cf. *Conseils et souvenirs réunis par les novices*). This one sentence contains the whole program of our life: To abandon ourselves to the Lord, that is, not to care about anything, because He loves us and takes care of everything. Only then true peace will begin to penetrate our souls and our hearts. We cannot free ourselves from that which threatens us, that which gives rise to fear; therefore, it is very important to remove these fears through a conscious act of abandoning ourselves to the Lord.

When St Paul asked Jesus to remove some kind of great difficulty from his life, Christ answered him that power is made perfect in weakness (cf. *2 Co* 12:8-9). St Thérèse wrote that *trust and faith are made perfect amidst fears*. So how great is the role of your fear in God's economy? It is there to provoke an act of faith within you. Fear is a trial of faith and that is why God allows it, so that you may grow in faith. Trust and faith are made perfect amidst fears.

Fear can contribute to illness in many people. Fear lies at the basis of neuroses and psychoses. *But it can be an outlet to total abandonment to God*. Everything depends on you. Fear is a challenge issued to you. What will you do with it? Will you allow yourself to be enslaved by its weight? Or, instead, will you try to perform acts of abandoning yourself to Him who is infinite power and infinite love. Everything that happens, is connected with our decision. We cannot rid ourselves of fear as an emotional state, at least not always. Fear, however, can become a factor that deepens our faith, just as each temptation can.

To St Margaret Marie Alacoque, the great apostle of the Sacred Heart of Jesus, Jesus said with unusual fervour: "Let me act". Christianity is a religion of grace, a religion which directs us towards allowing Christ to act, towards opening ourselves more and more to His work. What we are called to is that kind of openness which allows Christ to live fully within us. Then He can re-create you into His masterpiece, just as in the case of the Virgin Mary, who lived by faith, trust and complete abandonment to the Lord.

The basic principle of God's action is that *He does not want to impose on you*. If the door to your heart is closed, He will not want to force it open: "Jesus will do everything for me", wrote St Margaret Marie, "if only I allow Him to act in me. He will love in me, desire in me, supply all that I am lacking". *Abandoning oneself to God is the highest form of self-entrusting to Him, the highest form of reliance on the Lord*: "I no longer desire suffering or death", said St Thérèse of the Child Jesus. "However, I love them both; but it is love alone that attracts me... Now it is abandonment alone that guides me, I do not need any other compass! [...] I cannot ask ardently for anything else except for the perfect fulfilment of the will of the Good Lord in my soul without any obstacles from creatures" (*Manuscrits autobiographiques*). Thérèse admits: "It took me a long time before I was established in this degree of abandonment. Now I am there; God has placed me there. He took me into His arms and placed me there" (*The Yellow Notebook*, July 7ᵗʰ, In *St Thérèse of Lisieux, Her Last Conversations*, Washington, D.C. 1977, p.77).Your self-entrusting to God and accepting His will in everything, will be complete if you are able to say: *"I love everything you send upon me."*

The Jealous Love of God

God burns with a jealous love for you. It means that *He wants to be your only Lord, your only love* (cf. *Ex* 20:5; Deut 5:9). He calls us to conversion which always has two elements, turning 'to' and turning 'away from'. We are to turn away from everything that pushes us away from the only Lord, whom we belong to. We are to turn away from our egoism which desires securities, and which is deeply set in our souls. If you had formed some system of security and God had then caused your 'manna' to rot, then remember, He did this out of love. *God strips you of that which is your enslavement and which leads to lack of faith in His love*. He is the only Lord, yours and your 'manna's', that is to say, the Lord of your daily bread and your existence. Everything depends on Him. He, whether you acknowledge it or not, will remain the only Lord, but He is the Lord who loves you. He does not want you to get lost in a false kingdom of a false god because that kingdom will destroy you. You are His possession including everything you own; your body and soul, your work which is dependent on Him, your home which is His, your children who belong to Him, and your time which you often dole out to Him like a miser, despite the fact that all of your time also belongs to Him.

The gospel says that you cannot serve two masters. The word *douleuein* [to serve] in Greek means the type of servitude a slave is engaged in, for his master. A slave does not have time for himself. The master controls the slave's time completely and always. *You need to give God everything*; you need to know how to give Him, that which is His; that is the program of our conversion. *You must also accept His jealous love and accept Him as the only treasure, the only love.* The expression 'jealous love' contains the entire depth of God's love, because He is not jealous for His own advantage but for yours, jealous so that you will not get lost in servitude to false gods.

A person who reaches union with God and attains sanctity is one who has accepted Christ to the very end as the only love. There are two categories of believers: those who collect merits, and those who simply try to love. To love means not only to give but even more so to accept, to accept the love of another person.

To love God means to accept His love, His jealous love for you is a jealous and 'folly' love. This love wants to protect you from everything that may be a threat to your freedom and your faith.

The Lord burns with a jealous love for you. That love is God's torment; it is God's hunger for you, you who are His child, His possession. He will fight for you. His jealous love will sometimes be difficult, because sometimes you slip through His fingers and fall towards the abyss, often not even realising it. Therefore, sometimes God will have to shake you. He will have to give you 'difficult' graces, but that is so that He may save you, so that you may in the end entrust yourself to Him. – The jealous love of God.

Chapter 4

Faith as Acknowledging
One's Own Helplessness
and Awaiting Everything from God

In the light of faith, we can see our own helplessness and
await everything from God. Walter Kasper writes that according to the synoptic Gospels the meaning of faith is to
know one's own helplessness and to trust in the power of
God acting through Jesus (cf. *Einführung in den Glauben*,
Ch.5). A believer does not wait for anything from himself
but expects everything from the Lord.

It is only when we acknowledge, in the spirit of faith, our
own helplessness, that we become poor in spirit and allow
the power of God to act within us.

Evangelical morality is not only the morality of the
Decalogue, although that is its premise, but it is primarily
the morality of the Beatitudes, especially the morality of
the first Beatitude: "Blessed are the poor in spirit, for theirs
is the kingdom of heaven" (*Mt* 5:3). They are 'blessed', because it is they, the poor, who actually enter the Kingdom.

"Blessed are the Poor in Spirit"

He who seeks above all the kingdom of heaven, and therefore seeks sanctity, will find it and find everything else, that
is, all the spiritual and temporal gifts necessary for life.
"Blessed are the poor in spirit". They are attached to nothing, having nothing and awaiting everything from God. They
are blessed because there is room in their hearts for the
Lord. The kingdom of heaven belongs to them because they
have God. This is a joyous gospel about blessed people whose
hearts are free for the Lord.

You have faith to the extent of your being poor in spirit. The word 'poor', in the biblical sense, does not necessarily mean poverty in the material sense. For example, King David, a man placed at the top of a social scale, was poor in spirit. A person poor in spirit is one who is stripped of self-confidence. He is one who knows that he cannot count on himself, or on his own strength. This kind of person is orientated towards awaiting everything from God, and is not rooted in temporal things.

If you feel that you are strong in the sense that you possess natural abilities your faith cannot develop and deepen. That is why you have to experience your weakness; you have to realise that there are things you cannot do. This will be the call to faith. Your weakness, inability, and helplessness will become a crack through which the grace of faith will squeeze into your heart. *Through your injuries, God gives you the grace of deepening your faith.* Charles Péguy, a great convert, writes: "One sees unbelievable graces which penetrate the evil soul, and even the depraved soul. Even that, which seemed to be lost, is saved. However, one does not perceive that, which has been varnished, to be soaked, that which has been impermeable, to be permeated, and that which has been hardened, to be softened...

This is the source of so many deficiencies in the efficacy of grace. Grace, while bringing so many victories over the souls of the greatest sinners, often remains ineffective within the 'righteous'" (*Note conjointe sur M.Descartes et la philosophie cartésienne* – samedi 1er août 1914). "It is so, because these 'righteous' people, those mature in the evangelical sense, have no deficiencies; they are not wounded. They are powerful, strong, self-sufficient, and adult. Their moral skin, constantly intact," continues Péguy, "becomes their shell and armour of faultlessness. They do not present an opening which is caused by some kind of terrible wound, by some kind of unforgotten distress, by some kind of resentment they have not been able to overcome, by some kind of stitch which is not properly joined, by some kind of mortal fear, by some kind of invisible anxi-

58

ety at the back of their minds, by some kind of hidden bitterness, by some kind of fall which is always masked, by
some kind of scar which is badly healed. They do not reveal
that point of entry for grace. This, in essence, is their sin.
Since they are not wounded, they are no longer vulnerable.
Because they lack nothing, nothing is given to them. Lacking nothing, they cannot receive that which is everything.
*God's charity alone does not heal those who have no
wounds.*
It was because a man lay on the ground that a Samaritan picked him up... So he who has not fallen," continues
Péguy, "will never be picked up, and he who is not dirty, will
never be wiped clean." The so called self-righteous adults,
are impenetrable to grace.

Maybe even in your life there is a terrible unhealed sore,
maybe an unforgotten torment, maybe a resentment that
you have not been able to get over, maybe some kind of
hidden bitterness, which accompanies so many things in
this life, maybe some kind of disaster. You then think that
is the end, but this is not so.
All of this is to be your channel for grace. *God must
allow so many wounds, so many hard moments, so that
you feel weak and through this, you are open to grace.*
When you feel very painfully touched, remember that
this is a blessed pain, which makes room for grace to penetrate your armour of maturity and self-righteousness. All
of this is a chance for you to deepen your faith. Your weakness, through faith, lets the might of God dwell in you. God,
when coming closer to you, must make you weaker so that
you will need Him, so that as your faith and trust in Him
increases, you will seek support from Him.
You have to be humbled, for you are too great – and
wounding humbles. Hence, every wounding gives you
a chance to become more and more like an Evangelical child.
*Sometimes it will take many wounds to become a child
so that you will walk 'the little way'.*

The Might of God Needs the Weakness of Man

God, getting closer to man, weakens him. He does just the opposite of what we would expect.

You may believe that it is you who are approaching Him and that under those conditions you should become increasingly stronger and increasingly more able to get along by yourself. However, it is He who is coming closer to you and His approach makes you weaker, physically, mentally or spiritually. He does this in order to dwell in you with His might, *since it is your weakness that makes room for His might*. When you are weak, you cannot trust in yourself, you cannot believe in yourself and then the opportunity comes for you to turn to Him and to desire to rely on Him. So often you shield yourself against this greatest grace, *the grace of weakness*, but St Paul has already written: "for power is made perfect in weakness. I will rather boast most most gladly of my weaknesses, in order that the power of Christ may dwell with me... for when I am weak, then I am strong" (*2 Co* 12:9-10). *Your own power and strength must collapse sooner or later*. Strictly speaking, there is nothing you can call exclusively your own strength. Any kind of strength is a gift – a gift which you usually claim as your own; and that is why it must be taken from you.

Often St Maximillian Kolbe felt completely helpless during his unusual apostolic journeys. Frequently the climate was not suitable for his ailing lungs. His body did not tolerate well the tedious journeys across the sea and the humidity. These made it difficult for him to breathe. All of this, however, did not stop him from proclaiming the kingdom of the Immaculate, even though it seemed as if he would not survive another hour on the ship. Maybe at that time he spoke to Mary saying: "I cannot last another hour. How then shall I expand your kingdom?" – However, this weakness was his whole strength.

If God chooses to act through you, it will then be based on your weakness. If you try to be powerful and forceful in your apostolate, you become an anti-sign. *People do not want your power, your personal power*, since this is demeaning to them. God also, in order to make you his sign and to act through you, does not need your power. The very opposite is the case.

He needs your weakness. This idea was very clearly expressed back in the Old Testament with Gideon as an example (*Jg* 7:1-8,10). Gideon's enemy had one hundred and thirty-five thousand soldiers and Gideon had thirty-two thousand, four times less.

However, there were victories despite such a disproportion in history. For God, therefore, this disproportion was too small. He tells Gideon to reduce the number of his warriors. The first trial depended on reducing the army from thirty-two thousand to ten thousand. Now Gideon's army is thirteen times smaller. In the history of military strategy, victories do not happen with this kind of disproportion, however, man could still claim it as his own and attribute it to his own genius. Gideon is, therefore, still too strong and can count on his own abilities. God tries him once again; he tells him to reduce these ten thousand men to three hundred.

And now it is not clear whether the situation is dramatic or comical. It is really ludicrous to go against the enemy with such a number, when they are four hundred and fifty times stronger. In these circumstances, only God can be victorious, not Gideon. – And Gideon will march with this handful of men and will be victorious. This disheartening disproportion will not allow even the temptation for Gideon to claim it as his own. The whole situation is so absurd that it is as though God, were smiling, and saying: "You see, Gideon, you wanted to be victorious relying on your own abilities and the strength of your armies. Look, you are left with three hundred men against one hundred and thirty-five thousand of the enemy. What can you say to that?" Gideon trusted the Lord and was victorious; he had a victory, the like of which has never before been seen in history.

The Lord places His gift in a fragile, clay vessel *so that whatever we do comes from the power of God, not from us* (cf. *2 Co* 4:7). God stripped Gideon of his human power, made him small and weak, did something that in human terms seems absurd. Something like this can happen in your life. If there is within you thirty-two thousand elements of human power, God will make it ten thousand and then three hundred. You will then be truly weak, almost defeated, and that is how, being weak, you will be victorious. These will be victories not through your power but through the might of God.

The Poverty of Christ

Faith as an expression of poverty in spirit has its example in the life and person of Jesus.

To be poor means to be dependent. In the life of Jesus we see three moments, when His poverty becomes extreme. *God, becomes entirely dependent and shows Himself in his powerlessness, as if in defeat: these are Bethlehem, Calvary and the Most Blessed Sacrament.*

If poverty means dependence, then Jesus became completely dependent already in *Bethlehem*, where there was a situation of powerlessness, one could even say defeat, because Jesus was not accepted by His own people and had to be born in conditions which were inhumane. Every one of your experiences of powerlessness and the inability to cope with something is partaking in the powerlessness of Jesus.

Terrifying in its expression, *Calvary* is the second situation of the denudation of Jesus. Here, He also is unable to do anything to help Himself, as His hands, those hands which blessed the crowds, are now nailed to the cross, bleeding. He cannot use His feet, because those feet, which before had brought love and Good News, are now nailed down. Jesus on Calvary is stripped of everything. *The cross is an expression of the folly of God's love. Here, the nakedness of Jesus is extreme.*

Yet another expression of the nakedness of Jesus is the Most Blessed Sacrament. Here, there is also a situation of powerlessness and defeat, similar to that on Calvary. But of course, this only seems to be a defeat. Jesus is silent in the Most Blessed Sacrament, even when people pray to Him. In the tabernacle, He remains naked to the extent, that one can take Him out and move Him wherever one wants, one can accept Him as well as desecrate Him. Therefore one can do with Him whatever one wants, literally whatever one wants. *And this is the amazing mystery of the nakedness and poverty of Christ, His* kenosis, *His complete offering Himself to man.*

These three situations: Bethlehem, Calvary and the Most Blessed Sacrament, are situations in which the love of Jesus really reaches the point of folly by leading Him to extreme poverty.

But it is through this folly and this poverty that Jesus brings you your Redemption, brings you faith. God's being silent, His powerlessness, His 'defeat' is a scandal for the world, which wants a God full of visible power. The Cross was and continues to be a stumbling block for those who do not believe, but, for those who have faith, it is the highest power. Your cross, which is your nakedness and poverty, makes room for grace in you – room for the grace of faith.

To Acknowledge that Everything is a Gift

Faith is the acknowledgement of one's own helplessness, the belief that one owns nothing, that everything is a gift. It is the awaiting of all the gifts from God. The opposite of such a faith is pride. A proud person considers all these gifts as his own and attributes them to himself. He thinks that everything depends on him, as if the unceasing gift from God did not exist in his life.

Of course, faith is a difficult thing. To live in faith means to be born again, reborn to become poor in spirit and to regain the attitude of a child.

A gift should be accepted with such detachment that at any given moment you could return it. This is an astonishing paradox. We are gifted so that, in accepting God's gifts, we are ready to return them. The gesture of our readiness to return to God a gift we received, is a sign that we have not taken possession of it. It is an expression of acknowledgement of the truth that we possess nothing.

A gift returned to God comes back multiplied. Everything is a gift: your body and soul, wife, husband, children, what you have and what you do – everything belongs to the Lord. *Are you ready to return each of these gifts at any moment?*

The episode of the rich young man, who walked away sadly when the Lord suggested that he should give up material wealth, has its epilogue. After he left, Jesus talking about those who trust in their riches says: "My children, how hard it is to enter the kingdom of God!" (*Mk* 10:24).

Note that this young man fulfilled all the commandments. It appears from this that *it is not enough to fulfil the commandments*. It is about him and others like him that Jesus says, "It is easier for a camel to pass through the eye of a needle than for someone rich to enter the kingdom of God". It is a statement so strong that the Apostles, terrified by this, ask: "In that case, who can be saved?" (*Mk* 10:25-26).

That young man, who appeared to be open to God, was a slave to the worldly life, a slave to his own riches and to social status. St Luke speaks of him as an official, therefore we know that he held an important position (cf. *Lk* 18:18). All of this can come between a person and God and it can become such a great obstacle that for a person like the young man, it may be very difficult for him to be saved. Attachment to temporal reality, to that which God has created, to that which is only a gift and is not God Himself, can, through enslavement, not only hinder but also make our salvation impossible.

During my journey to San Giovanni Rotondo to see Father Pio I met a scientist who was also travelling there, in

order to ask Father Pio to bless his work. He came with two
volumes of a published work which he called his *opus vitae*
– life's work. During confession, he presented them to Father Pio and asked for his blessing. Father Pio's reaction
was frightening. First and foremost, he expressed his astonishment: "This is your *opus vitae?* This is your life's
work?" He took the two volumes into his hands and repeated,
"Is this your *opus vitae?* Does it mean that you have lived
these sixty years to write these two books?" he almost
shouted. "Is this *opus vitae?* Is this what you have lived for?
And where is your faith?"

Then he softened, as if he had seen the naïveté of this
man and with the gentleness of a father he asked, "I'm sure
you put a great deal of effort into it, didn't you? I'm sure
there were a lot of sleepless nights. And how is your health?
Well, yes, a heart attack. All this in the name of ambition,
to create this type of *opus vitae?* See," Padre Pio continued:
"what idols and attachments mean. If you had done the
same, but for God, everything would be different. You
claimed everything as your own, that this was **your** *opus
vitae,* **your** own work". The end of this confession was also
in Father Pio's style. He raised his voice again: "If this is all
you came with, *va via,* please leave". Father Pio was *'brusco'*
as the Italians say, which means harsh, but behind this
harshness lay a great love for each person and each peni-
tent. This was a man who loved; and love is powerful. It
was Father Pio's love that was the reason for this shocking
conversation, and together with confession, became the real
turning point in the life of this scientist who then really
started to think differently and look at the world differently.

Abraham, the father of our faith, received a miraculous
gift, when he was very old, a son was born to him. This was
the greatest joy for him to receive one of the greatest gifts
in human terms: a son, an heir. Parents usually claim children for themselves and maybe Abraham succumbed to this
temptation. When, however, God told Abraham that He
wanted him to sacrifice his son, Abraham agreed. He also
agreed to give up the gift he had received in a way that was
most traumatic for him. What would have happened if

Abraham had not wanted to give up his son, if he had rebelled and held fast to the belief that God's request was too
cruel? What would have happened then? Isaac would have
had to die!

The circumstances of his death would have been unimportant. Whether it would have been because of sickness,
or during a battle, or being devoured by a wild animal, he
would have had to be taken away from Abraham because
he would have stood between Abraham and God. Isaac would
have then become an obstacle preventing Abraham's total
devotion to God in faith. Not giving up his son would have
meant that Abraham claimed him for himself. Taking possession of a gift means destroying it, as if it were a blow
aimed at oneself and at the gift itself. Abraham, in giving
up his son, not only regained him but more than that, received a gift multiplied – the grace of sanctity in which his
son also shared. Abraham and Isaac were the first Holy
Patriarchs of the Old Covenant.

The Seeds of Distrust

When we analyse the mechanism of how evil is begotten
in humankind, we notice that the foundation of evil lies in
lack of simplicity and lack of childlike trust in God. This is
how it has been from the beginning of the history of humankind, from the moment when our first parents, Adam
and Eve were placed in a situation that tried their faith.
At the origins of human history lies the trial of trust. It is
as if God posed the question, "Do you trust Me? Do you
have the simplicity and trust of a child towards Me?"

The Bible clearly states that the first human was at-
tacked by Satan in this very way. Satan did not tempt the
first parents to evil, as it were. He did not tempt them directly to sin. What he did was that he sowed distrust in a
perfectly psychological way, in a way particular only to him.
He did not say, "Be unfaithful; be disobedient". – No, he
tried to convince our first parents that there is no love, sin-
cerity and truth in God. At the foundation of the mecha-

nism of evil in the Original Sin lies the distrust that was sown which caused a great retention of impressions. A person who does not trust begins to feel threatened.

A person, whom I do not trust, becomes a threat to me and I begin to fear him. The sin of distrust brings threat and fear. This fear, which is spoken about at great length in psychology and psychiatry, becomes very often the source of human suffering.

If we are not free from sin, then we cannot be free from that which stems from it; anxiety, fear, the feeling of being threatened. We are also tempted by these seeds of distrust. If this distrust is towards God, then we feel as if we are locked in a cage; and life in a 'cage of threat" becomes something terrible.

Sin destroys a person also because he is destroyed by the fear that accompanies sin. The feeling of being threatened becomes the final blow to us, since one of the most basic emotional needs for a person is the need for security. From this we can conclude that fear, which we do not fight against, is our fault.

The redeeming works of Christ continue. Through faith, we are incorporated into redemption which includes not only our sin, but everything that pertains to it. Therefore, fear as well as the feeling of being threatened, becomes a part of the Redemption. Jesus, dying on the Cross, redeemed us from fear and the from the feeling of being threatened, just as He redeemed us from sin. All our lives should be orientated towards an increasingly greater openness towards the redeeming action of Christ. Grace flows continuously from the Cross so that we may be saved from sin as well as from fear.

How are you to fight this fear that surrounds us? If you fight it directly, this will end in a fiasco. There is only one unfailing way: *Open yourself up to the redeeming action of Christ through such faith, like an 'Evangelical child'.* You must believe that Jesus redeemed you from everything that threatens you, that you are truly free. You should say to yourself: There is no threat, since He has redeemed me and has freed me from everything. I need only to accept this. *Faith is the acceptance, the process of accepting the redeeming action of Christ.*

When Peter was going through one of the gates of the temple, he met a crippled man who begged him for alms. Peter then said to him: "I have neither silver nor gold, but I will give you what I have: in the name of Jesus Christ the Nazarene, walk" (*Ac* 3:6). And the crippled man rose. This begging, crippled man was helpless and he expected a great deal. He also must have had a lot of childlike faith, for he received more than he expected.

You, who are crippled by fear by a sense of being threatened, do not necessarily have to be healed as immediately as that crippled man. This will depend on the degree of your faith, on whether you really have the faith of a child. You can be healed instantly or healed gradually. This crippled man, who symbolises your situation, will be lifted gradually by the hand of Christ, ever higher, and in this way, you will slowly begin to rise. Your gradual lifting is also a redeeming action of Christ.

It is difficult to believe, but it is even harder not to believe. Try, as often as possible, to realise that you are not alone. Christ, who has redeemed you, is with you. Try to oppose those fears, which depress you, with a childlike feeling of your own helplessness. Say to Jesus, "I know that you want to cleanse me from this leprosy, I know that You have already redeemed me from it".

Did you know that you could be a witness to a miracle? Christ said, "If you had faith like a mustard seed, you would say to this mulberry tree, 'Be uprooted and planted in the sea', and it would obey you" (*Lk* 17:6). Then you would see that the unlimited power of God is in faith, which in the eyes of the world is such a small 'nothing', just like a mustard seed, the smallest of seeds. You would see that faith opens you to the redeeming works of Christ, and in a miraculous way removes fear. Then, suddenly, you would feel that you are a free person.

You are called to freedom and peace through faith that opens you to Christ's Redemption. Therefore you must continually be converted to this faith, because faith is a continuous process. This process deepens itself through continuing acts of faith, arising most often in the face of a threat. *By stirring then within yourself acts of faith, you will in every situation entrust yourself as a child into the arms of the loving Father.*

The essence of the 'little way' of St Thérèse of the Child Jesus is found in the attitude of a child free from all fear thanks to *childlike trust*. At the origin of mankind, sin arose because of the sowing of distrust. The 'little way', which emphasises the importance of trust and childlike faith in God, is both an antidote to distrust and an exact antithesis of that event. The program of the 'little way' strikes at the very root of evil which is caused by lack of trust. Those seeds of distrust towards God are in large measure, directly at the source of all of your sins and at the source of your existential or emotional torment, and indirectly at the source of your physical torment. *If you trust in the Lord, you will sever the root of that which destroys you.*

Believe that He loves you. The trial of faith for Adam and Eve was not that difficult, but the Bible speaks also of the terrible trial which God had given Abraham. He received the terrifying order to kill his own son. It was so easy at that time to accept the seeds of distrust; not to trust but to rebel. Abraham, however, despite the darkness that surrounded him, trusted.

How important is this complete trust in God, the childlike trust in Him, whom we wound most deeply with our sin of distrust.

If you have ever been in a situation when someone whom you loved very much, lost trust in you, then you know how painful this is. This is not an ordinary situation of human friendship injured by distrust; this is a situation of a human distrusting the infinite love of God. How great must be the pain inflicted to this Love by our lack of trust. The words: "I am afraid to turn everything over to God" hurt like a slap in the face, because it is as if you were saying to God: "I don't trust You, I do not know what You are going to do to me". If a small child were to say this to his mother, it would be extremely painful for her. How great must be the pain, which God experiences, when man slaps Him with such lack of faith!

Distrust, in a certain way, is worse than sin *because it is the root and the source of sin.* If you do not want to trust, if your Enemy is able to engraft distrust in your heart, then consequences will have to follow – fear, the feeling of being threatened, and suffering associated with this.

Only through the consequences of this evil will you see how far you have strayed. Suffering, fear and the feeling of being threatened will be an incessant call for you to be converted. You will continue to carry the burden of fear until you will be converted, until you become like a child who simply entrusts himself into his loving Father's arms.

"A patient should be treated for as long as it takes until he learns to pray", wrote L. Szondi. This does not refer to repeating simple prayers. It refers to an attitude of deep prayer, *the trusting prayer of a child who surrenders himself fully into the arms of the Father.*

Spiritual Poverty as a Childlike Attitude

Faith as the acknowledgement of one's own helplessness and awaiting everything from God *means having the attitude of a child.* A child fully acknowledges that it has nothing, that it is unable to do anything. It is filled with expectations and faith that everything that it needs it will receive: "[...] Unless you turn and become like little children you will never enter the kingdom of Heaven", said the Lord (*Mt* 18:3). Conversion to the attitude of a child is an imperative condition for entering the kingdom of God. At some point in time you must become like a child; trusting, humble, awaiting everything from the Lord. If you do not become a child here on earth, then this will have to happen in Purgatory. The state of being childlike is absolutely imperative, not only for sanctity but also for redemption.

The 'Evangelical child' awaits everything from God, literally everything. The childlike dimension of our faith means not depending on ordinary human calculations, but it means the stirring of a hunger for something, which a child would call a surprise. It is being hungry for a miracle. Your spirit is young only as far as you remain a child. A person can be very old at the age of twenty. On the other hand, one can be eighty years old and remain young thanks to one's childlike spirit. God is always young, and the Church instituted by Christ is always young, that is why She needs the "young in spirit". He needs the child within you, who is able to believe everything. An *old person*, someone who relies on his own calculations, who lists pros and cons, *limits the possibility for God to act and sets limits on His love and mercy*. Constant calculating and predicting if one will be successful or not is a trait of old age.

A child grasps for the moon and believes that it will get it – and God wants to give you more than the moon. He wants to give you His kingdom, but if you do not become a child, His hands will be tied.

Children are also the typical Evangelical "violent ones" that Jesus speaks about, that are taking the heavenly kingdom by force (cf. *Mt* 11:12). When a child wants to get into his home, then he has to get in. He will continue to pound with his fists or kick with his feet until he will be let in. Jesus said: "[...] knock and the door will be opened to you" (*Lk* 11:9).

If we knew how to knock at the doors, which are closed before us, so that we would pound to get in the way children do, then the doors would have to be opened. *God needs your childlike faith in order to perform miracles in you and through you, as nothing is impossible for God*: "Everything is possible for one who has faith" (*Mk* 9:24). Everything is possible for one who is an 'Evangelical child'.

The Gospel tells us of two Annunciations: the Annunciation to Zechariah and the Annunciation to Mary. Zechariah showed himself to be a man who was old not only in age but also in spirit, a person who tied up God's hands, for he was unable to believe in miracles. In order for him to believe He, had to be touched with a different, painful for him, miracle, which was the taking away of his ability to speak. This kind of spiritual 'old age' in a person, who is unable to believe in a miracle, is something terrible for God. A person lacking the attitude of a child, usually as if in advance, negates the efficacy of his prayers, since within him there is something of Zechariah's attitude. This 'righteous before God', faultless old man had no heir and asked for a child. He prayed, but actually at the same time, did not believe that God would listen to him. When the angel announced to him, "[...] your prayer has been heard. Your wife Elizabeth will bear you a son [...]" (*Lk* 1:13), it seems that he did not want to accept this son, did not believe this miracle. All this time he had prayed for a son and when God heard him, he did not believe it. He raised an argument against his own prayer: "For I am an old man, and my wife is advanced in years" (*Lk* 1:18). He was an 'old' man, no longer believing the Lord.

We often resemble Zechariah. Referring to a certain priest, A. Pronzato relates how he called the parishioners to pray for rain and then severely reprimanded them saying: "You came to ask for rain; where then are your umbrellas?"

The second Annunciation is the Annunciation to Mary, who is so much a child, that she is ready to accept everything. Mary was so much at His disposal, that God could have 'conjured up' extraordinary things for her. She would have accepted everything, believed everything, *for her attitude toward God was permeated with the true power of a childlike spirit.* Do you think sometimes that it is the children and not the old people that rule the world? – Yes, children rule the world, since *a person who has a childlike spirit has 'power over God'. God cannot resist him*; He cannot deny the eyes of a child filled with true faith and trust.

Peter, while walking towards Christ on the water, at a certain point stopped being a child. He started to analyse that situation: I walked so far because the surface of the water was smooth, but here comes a wave. Can I go on? He started to reason in a purely human way and his faith vanished. Peter at this moment stopped being a child; that is why he started sinking. He turned out to be an old man and would later remain old for a long time. That is why he later betrayed Jesus.

It can be said that you sin because you are 'old', for being old in spirit closes you off from grace and ties up God's hands. God is young and wants to conjure up the moon for you. Was this not the moon for St Thérèse of Lisieux when He gave snow to her the day she took her veil? God loves this kind of attitude, the kind that does not see limits, and this is the attitude of a child. It sees no limits on possibilities, it is persevering to the point of folly, it is open to that which is new – a child is able to believe.

God is always young and always amazes man. Experiencing God is experiencing an amazing reality. A person with an attitude of an 'Evangelical child' is able to be amazed. This kind of person looking at the world can be amazed by everything that surrounds him. *In the moment that you cease to be a child before the Lord, there will be a crisis in your spiritual life, you will begin to regress; you will stop believing and loving.*

Only two categories of people believe in miracles – saints and children. Actually, this is one category, as saints are children in spirit. *God, Himself, in Jesus Christ became a child.* He became a child not only in Bethlehem, but also on the Cross, where He was completely defenceless and dependent upon people for everything. This God, who became a child, wants our helplessness and weakness to lead us towards the complete abandonment of ourselves to Him. He wants to lead us to a limitless trust in His mercy.

The parable of the Prodigal Son should really be called the Parable of the Merciful Father. The older son, one of the three characters of the drama, does not arouse in us good feelings towards him; he is jealous and impertinent towards his father. Our sympathy lies with the prodigal son, the one who returned, especially because he is like us. In the figure of the prodigal son, we almost spontaneously find ourselves. Is his attitude, however, truly evangelical?

The Gospel says that the return to his father was a calculated one. He returned with the hope that it would be better with his father, since he knew that his father paid his hired workers more than the master whom he served. "I will arise and go to my father, and I will say to him, 'I [...] am no longer worthy to be called your son; treat me as one of your hired servants" (*Lk* 15:18-19). The parable about the prodigal son seems unfinished. There is the further episode in the *drama of the prodigal son; the drama caused by the fact that there is more of attitude of a hired help in him than that of a child.* He wants to be considered by his father as someone with whom a bargain could be struck, just like those who agreed to a daily wage with the landowner (*Mt* 20:1-26). If, therefore, the prodigal son does not return as a child, but as a hired worker, then he will certainly leave again for a second, third... or many more times.

The son who has the soul of a hired worker cannot be amazed by love. *The prodigal son did not perceive the wounding of his father, did not see his pain; he saw only his own misfortune* and sought a way out from it. In the parable of the hired workers, it was the workers of the last hour that were amazed by the landowner's generosity, and not those who had been hired for a certain sum. *Only an 'Evangelical child' can be amazed,* since amazement implies two contrasting realities. A child knows that it is such a small 'nothing' yet it is constantly being gifted with something great. This great contrast between one's own smallness and of being richly gifted gives rise to childlike wonder.

A person becomes a Christian when he becomes a child, *when the folly of God the Father's love begins to amaze him.* We discover here a new aspect of the evangelical child – a certain *identity between a child and a contrite sinner.*

What does contrition depend on? Contrition is a sorrow, a sorrow in the face of the Cross, when conscious of your own wretchedness and sinfulness, you look upon the Cross and Jesus' wounds, when you try in your soul to kiss those wounds, which you inflicted on Jesus. That is contrition. There was no such contrition in the prodigal son. *Only then, when being contrite you kiss the wounds of Jesus and believe in His love, do you return to God with the attitude of a child.* Only such a return has any sense. Never return to God as a hired worker for you will betray Him again.

We see true contrition in the sinful woman when she meets Jesus in the home of the Pharisee, Simon. Her simplicity, spontaneity and authentic contrition are the evidence of her attitude of an evangelical child. In order to express her contrition to Jesus, she came up to Him, not caring what people might think, poured ointment, bathed His feet with her tears, and wiped them with her hair (*Lk* 7:38). This is the simplicity, spontaneity and contrition of a sinner who is an 'Evangelical child'. Those who truly love God are the *contrite sinners*, whom much is forgiven, and *saints*, since they both have the nature of a child. *They are able to be amazed by the love of God; by the folly of His love for them.* It is not hired workers but children; not those who accumulate approval and try to enter into deals with God, but those who believe in His Mercy. Indeed, only a child has such faith!

Part Two

The Dynamism of Faith

*Faith, as an expression of our relationship
with God, is a dynamic phenomenon as a result
of a constant process of change. This process is
brought about through God's initiative and
through man's answer, revealing abandonment
to God. God tears down our stability. Through
difficult situations, He undermines our
abandonment to Him; through trials of faith
and the experience of our nakedness, God gives
our trust a new dynamism. Difficult situations,
internal as well as external prompt our
conversion. They impart dynamism to our
reliance on Christ, our dependence on Him for
support, our entrusting ourselves to Him and
our awaiting everything from God.*
*Faith, can become a buried talent if we do
not grow in it, but God will not allow this. He
does not want our faith to become stiff. That is
why, in the hope of deepening and imparting
dynamism to faith, God allows difficult
situations to take place which forces us to make
choices continually. The dynamism of faith
becomes reality through trials which polarise
human attitudes. This leads to either a crisis
of faith or to its evident intensification. Our*

faith is incessantly changing. A year ago we believed differently regarding the intensity of our faith, and in a year we will believe still differently. Hence, the very important question arises. Is our faith growing or is it dwindling? We are not so much faithful as we are becoming faithful, not so much Christians as we are becoming Christians, not so much really living the Gospel, as we are trying to live up to it.

Chapter 1

Conversion as a Dimension of Faith

Conversion is a permanent and basic dimension of faith. Conversion prevents our faith from becoming static and enables it to undergo a permanent process of deepening itself. Conversion as a dimension of faith, is not as much a single act, as it is a process. It means a change in our way of thinking and the apparent transformation of our inner attitudes. During the process of conversion, we turn away from evil and we turn to God. Turning away from evil means not only turning away from sin alone, but also from its source which is unruly self-love.

Whenever Jesus reproached His Apostles, it was almost always due to their lack of faith. Jesus would often reproach them for not believing or having too little faith. In this, one can perceive an Evangelical paradox – it was those who followed Jesus, who believed in Him, that He reproached for their lack of faith and He does this many times. *The purpose of questioning the Apostle's faith was for their conversion*. You have to question your own faith. You have to be convinced that your faith should constantly grow and that its present condition will not suffice. This follows the principle that what you have achieved today will not be sufficient for tomorrow.

A Happy Fault

Our faith should develop through the permanent process of our conversion. Christ's rising from the dead meant that there is no ultimate failure in our life, that no life is doomed and that no evil is final. This is stated in the offertory of the former Liturgy of the Mass: "God, who miraculously created the dignity of human nature and even more miraculously restored it". God would not allow evil if He were not able to extract good from it. Our sin can become a 'happy fault' which is mentioned in the Liturgy of Holy Saturday. *God can turn every one of our faults into a 'felix culpa' – a happy fault.* It is a fault, which will remind us and show us in the light of faith, how much we are loved by the One who died and has risen for us. Not every fault becomes a happy fault. There are times when you do not return to Christ immediately after the fall, and you may even become more hardened, intractable. It is then that the real tragedy takes place because in this situation God is unable to forgive you.

All of your sins and infidelities should become happy faults but this can happen only if you are contrite and you long for forgiveness. That is why God, in his desire to help you and to overcome your obstinacy, always approaches you first, so that He may induce you to desire forgiveness.

God, who does not remember the wounds inflicted by us, constantly opens His Heart to man. He does it in many ways. He often reveals Himself to us and calls upon us through saints, whom He fills with his own, Divine love, or through the ministers of the Word and of the Sacraments, especially the Sacrament of Reconciliation.

The confessor of Charles de Foucauld, Father Huvelin, who lead him onto the path of conversion, said that God gave him the grace of an unusually fervent desire to absolve people from their sins. This longing to grant absolution, which God granted to Father Huvelin upon those occasions, revealed God's own constant and insatiable desire to forgive our sins. This is why you should fight with your sadness.

If you strayed from God, regardless of how far you have wandered away, you can always return. *After every fall, remember that He is waiting. When you return and ask His forgiveness, you make Him happy because you allow Him to love you through forgiveness.*

All your infidelities and sins will become happy faults if they help you know the Mercy of the Lord more deeply. They will become happy faults if they make you more trustful and humble, trusting the Lord more, and yourself less. You will grow in faith after they have been forgiven.

Your transgressions will become happy faults if the knowledge that you have hurt Jesus will pour new life into your love for Him. They will become happy faults if this knowledge will deepen your desire to give yourself over to Him – so that your heart may beat exclusively for Him just as His wounded Heart beats exclusively for you.

The Consequences of Evil

The unusual love that God has toward sinners and God's pedagogy toward us is shown in the parable of the Prodigal Son. If our faith becomes lukewarm and has no expression, God can allow us to fall. God does not want evil but may want its consequences, since the consequences of evil impart grace and the call to be converted. This can be seen very clearly in the example of the Prodigal Son. In Christ's parable, there is a father who loves, and two sons who do not love. The fact that the elder son does not love is clearly seen at the end of the parable when he shows his impertinence towards his father and jealousy toward his brother. The younger son also does not love his father. He does not leave his father for a short time but for always. The father did not oppose his son's leaving, although he could have. He let him take his share and leave, for love cannot be forced upon anyone. We know the consequences of the son's leaving his father's house. We know that he sunk lower into decline, and that life was increasingly more difficult for him.

In our commentary, we can try to find out certain elements that were not directly revealed in the parable. We can, for example, assume that the father found out through his servants what was going on with his youngest son; that he was starving, had nowhere to live and was a downtrodden tramp. Let us assume that the father, forthrightly or secretively, sent a servant to his son, with a bag of money in wanting to save him from this kind of downtrodden life. This would have given the son the possibility to live a normal life or also a life of debauchery. Would this type of constant help from the father cause the return of the son someday? Everything seems to indicate that it would not have. That means that a father, who loves his son, should not shield him from the evil consequences of his own deeds, despite the pain felt in the father's heart.

As a consequence of the evil committed by the Prodigal Son, two people are 'crucified,' the father, because of the pain he feels over his son's life of misery and failure, as well as the son himself as a result of his own failures. A father who loves his son should however wait until the evil is fulfilled and the consequences begin to take effect, even if there is risk involved. It was these consequences of sin, that wounded the son's self-love and inclined him to come back. We know that the time came when the measure of evil was full, when the downfall of the son was not only a moral failure in all its depth, but it also brought the ultimate disgrace. He wanted to fill his stomach with husks which were pig-feed, and according to the Palestinians the pigs were considered unclean animals. Therefore, this is the symbol of hitting the very bottom, it couldn't have been worse. And then the consequences of evil began taking effect. It was so bad for the son that he had a calculated, cold thought that it would be worth his while to return to his father, because his father treated his servants and hired workers better than the master for whom he had worked. It was not love for his father that decided the return of the Prodigal Son, but only simple, mercenary self-love, a cold calculation that it would be better for him – not for the father.

Upon returning, he sees his father running out to meet him, he finds himself in his father's arms and sees tears of joy in his father's eyes. Then he is clothed in the most beautiful cloak, receives a ring and sees that his father is preparing a feast for him. *Only then there is a chance that the son will discover his father's love*. That is how the consequences of evil may be connected with grace. God may want them so that they lead us to conversion. Sometimes only a failure and the suffering it entails are able to shock a person and lead to our conversion. Conversion requires contrition of heart and longing for forgiveness. God, who wants us to achieve the contrition and longing, runs out to meet us first. In his desire to forgive he lowers Himself so drastically that, as saints say, he sometimes becomes as if a beggar calling out for help.

The scene of suicide of an assistant commissioner Scobie, the main character in Graham Green's book "The Heart of the Matter" is shocking. In the last moments of his life, after he had taken a lethal dose of pills, the dying commissioner seems to hear that 'Someone' is desperately searching for him and calling him. He hears calls for help, a cry of distress, groans of pain. Responding to this call, Scobie manages to drag back, through infinite distance, the remaining consciousness to give an answer which will save him: 'Good God, I love...'

Roles seem to be paradoxically changed. It is not Scobie who is asking for help. It is God, who has identified Himself with the wretched man and calls for help ...for Himself. In the last moment of Scobie's life God calls out to him: "help me forgive you, allow me to save you!"

We Cannot Know Christ
if We do not Know Ourselves

We first have to admit to our sin for it to become a happy fault. St John in his Gospel tells us about Christ's promise that the Consoler, the Holy Spirit, when he comes, will convince the world about sin (cf. *Jn*:16:8). Therefore, one of the functions of the Holy Spirit, which descends on the world, *is to convince us of our sin.* This is the initial grace, fundamental to our interior life, which is granted to us by the Holy Spirit so that we can be convinced of the fact that we are sinners.

It is not enough, however, for us to accept this first grace of the Holy Spirit. If we would come to know only the reality of our sin, then it could ruin us. Our lives would solely become weighed down to the limit by our own evil; our lives would be marked with restlessness, stress and sorrow. There has to be an opening within us for further gifts of the Spirit, for the *discovery through faith of God's love for us*.

Pope John Paul II in his homily, in Plac Zwycięstwa in Warsaw, said the memorable words: "A man cannot be completely understood without Christ. Or rather: a man cannot understand himself completely without Christ", (Warsaw, 2nd June 1979). This means that if we do not take into consideration that Christ has entered into our lives, our perception of ourselves is reduced and therefore is false. If the Holy Spirit shows us that we are sinners and we do not discover Christ who loves us, then we could break down. Certain relations are so important to man that they seem to belong to his essence. Love is one of those relations. We cannot come to know ourselves without Christ, because *without Christ we cannot come to know that we are loved*, that we have been redeemed and chosen. The fact of being chosen, this love becomes an integral part of our 'self' and we cannot fight against this.

There is a second part to the truth spoken of above: *We cannot know Christ without coming to know ourselves*. We cannot comprehend who God is, we cannot believe in His greatness and His love for us if we first do not uncover the truth about ourselves.

If Christ loved us because we are worthy of love, it would not be meaningful. Man, even one without faith, is able to love someone who is worthy. Christ's love, as God's *agape*, is love which comes down from on high and loves that which is unworthy so that it may become worthy. *The more clearly we see our sinfulness, the more honestly we admit to it, the more we will rediscover Christ and fully believe in Him*. This is the paradox of faith, we cannot know Christ without coming to know ourselves. That is why it can be said that only saints really know Christ since they came to know themselves thoroughly and saw the enormity of their own sinfulness. This allowed them to discover the folly of God's love, which they sometimes expressed in their prayers by saying, "Lord, it is a folly that you love me, such a great sinner, so much!" *The moment of astonishment*, the characteristic trait seen in every authentic religious experience, can be seen here. A person who recognises that he is a sinner and believes in God's love, starts to see that God is truly 'crazy' in His love for him.

In the Face of One's Own Evil

The fight for faith as the process of conversion, entails overcoming hurry, restlessness, stress and especially sadness. *Sadness is an evident indication of self-love severing the very roots of faith, the roots of abandonment to God.* This concerns sadness that appears in situations of temporal difficulties, when something is taken away from us or we lose something. But even more so it concerns the sadness that comes about in the face of spiritual difficulties, when we fail, when we are unfaithful. Sorrow has a paralysing effect on our faith. After a fall, we should not feel down in spirit, since we hurt God more in this way, than by the sin itself. Moreover, saints say *that after a fall we are to expect graces greater than before the fall*.

To fight to accept defeats and failures in our lives we should include even the smallest matters. St Maximillian when playing chess with his brothers genuinely liked to lose. He turned away from self-love so that he could fully turn toward the Lord.

Try, in the light of faith, to look at your own imperfections in such a way that you are not saddened by them: Christ accepts you as you are. You can go to Him with all your imperfections and weaknesses. He will repair what you have done wrong and complete all that you lack.

Here you face an unusually important dilemma. On the one hand you are to reject the evil, which is within you, and on the other hand you are to accept yourself. You cannot love your imperfection itself, yet you can only want its consequences. The only purpose of this imperfection is that you can become ever more humble, trusting and faithful. The fact that you sin should not surprise you. Rather in the spirit of humbleness, you should be surprised that you don't fall. If you are surprised or discouraged because of falls, that means that you trusted in your own strength instead of allowing yourself to be carried in Jesus' arms: "But in one act of love, even *unfelt* love", stresses St Thérèse of the Child Jesus: "all is repaired [...]" (*Letter to Céline*, October 20th 1888). One should "not to become discouraged over one's faults", said the Saint, "for children fall often, but they are too little to hurt themselves very much" (*The Yellow Notebook*, August 6th 1897). St Thérèse of Lisieux really liked to entrust her faults and infidelities to Jesus. In this way she said that she wanted to attract His mercy, for He came to sinners and not to the righteous. How important all this is to us who are saddened by our falls.

"What does it matter, dear Jesus, if I fall at each moment?" writes St Thérèse: "I see my weakness through this and this is a great gain for me [...] You can see through this what I can do and now You will be more tempted to carry me in Your arms [...]" (*Letter to Céline*, April 26th 1889).

As we approach our goal, which is God, it seems to get further and further away. This is normal and proper. Thérèse, seeing herself getting increasingly distant from God, was not saddened by this at all: "Oh, how happy I am to see myself imperfect and to have such need of God's mercy at the moment of my death!" (*The Yellow Notebook*, July 29th 1897).

If you feel that you are sinful and weak, you have a special right to Jesus' arms because He is the Good Shepherd, who looks for lost sheep and those who are weak and helpless and who can't keep up with the flock. Allow Jesus to take you upon His shoulders. Allow Him to love. Believe in His love.

To have the right to rest upon His shoulders, you must be humble. You must admit and believe that you are a sinner, weak and helpless. You must, at the same time, believe in His love, that He takes you upon His shoulders because of the very fact that you are a sinner, weak and helpless. Faith will make you grateful for His never-ending love for you – a sinner, weak and helpless in the temporal life as well as in spiritual life.

"The Sacrament of Conversion"

Always, when you approach the sacrament of penance which can be called the sacrament of conversion, with true contrition, your faith has a great opportunity for growth. The sacrament of Penance often does not perform its true role in our life because it becomes routine and common-place with lack of preparation and disposition. You forget that penance, not only the Eucharist, is a particular channel for grace and a special time for your meeting with Christ. Maybe you also forget to pray for your confessor or spiritual director so that he may also become a more perfect instrument of God and an assistant in the process of your conversion.

Take a deep look within yourself. *Examine your conscience* and see what your life is directed to, what is most valuable to you and *who Jesus Christ is to you*. Primarily, you should confess from this basis. "Who is Jesus Christ to you?" What is your fundamental choice? Did you really ultimately choose Him? This is where the confession of sins should begin, for this consideration is most important. If you did not choose Christ, then your other sins are the consequences of this fundamental fault.

There can be various kinds of sin. There are sins committed and sins of negligence. And the sins of negligence are the worst. Among these is the sin of abandonment – *you abandon Christ, leave Him and give Him only a small corner in your heart*. This is your greatest evil. This compromise and lack of radicalism shows that Christ does not represent the greatest value in your life, that to you He is not everything, that your faith is always luke-warm.

Of the five conditions of the sacrament of Penance, the most important one is the *act of contrition*. How do you spend your time before confession? It is contrition that should directly prepare you for the meeting with Christ, for it can best open you to this channel of grace, which is the sacrament of conversion. Maybe you do not fully appreciate that the time you take in preparing for the sacrament of Penance is priceless. This time should be primarily spent on awakening contrition. *Contrition* is your attitude in the face of the Cross, the feeling that you wounded Christ with your sin, and that you desire God's forgiveness and the repair of evil. The fruitfulness of the sacrament of Penance depends on your contrition becoming ever deeper. *You cannot be converted until you are truly and fully contrite*.

One could say that two types of religiousness exist: one of them could be called 'egocentric' and the other 'theocentric'. In the first case, a person focuses on himself. He does not consider God but only his own situation. In order to be right in the face of God he goes to confession with the thought of cleansing himself, for his sin is a burden. For a person such as this, confession can become his own 'aspirin' for a painful conscience, a pill which is to placate him and return his good feelings about himself. This is a constant concentration upon oneself. This kind of person, when receiving absolution, leaves the confessional maybe not completely sad, but not happy either. This is because he is still concentrating on the evil of which he had just rid himself.

When we look at Judas, we can discover in his behaviour after betraying Jesus, many elements of confession. There is an examination of conscience because Judas thinks about what he had done and realises his own evil. Sorrow appears here as well, Judas is truly sorry. He even wants to change; hence he intends to make reparation for his sin. There is also a confession of sin when Judas goes to the chief priests and says: "I have sinned in betraying innocent blood" (*Mt* 27:4). He even makes satisfaction for his sin when he throws back at the chief priests the 30 pieces of silver which he had received from them. He does not want blood money. Actually, you can see almost everything which takes place in confession in Judas' behaviour and attitude. There is only one thing, the most important thing, missing. That is *faith in Jesus' mercy* (cf. L. Evely, *Le chemin de joie*, 116). That is why Judas' 'confession' is so sad, tragic and ended with despair and suicide.

Our confession should be a confession like Peter's: he believed in the mercy of Christ and concentrated not so much on his own sin but on forgiveness. A person with the 'theocentric' religious attitude does not dwell as much on his own sin. He considers sin as an advantage in discovering God's mercy through faith. Going into the confessional, he thinks primarily about the fact that he hurt Christ and wants to renew a friendship, which he wounded. Through contrition and sorrow, he wants to allow Jesus to forgive him and through this bring Him joy: "You crucified Christ," the Holy Curate from Ars (St Jean Marie Vianney) would say: "but when you go to confess, you go to free our Lord from the Cross".

If you wound Christ, then His wounds bleed. You should therefore take part in the sacrament of Penance so that these wounds can heal. *You should come because of Him, not to pacify yourself, but to invoke His happiness* of shaping within you a new-born person. This is brought about through sacramental graces.

Some feel guilty that after confession they do not improve. Maybe even you think that confession should serve to make you better and if you do not become better, then you feel that your confession is senseless. Maybe you feel that if you are supposed to be a better person and you do not become one, then it is better not to go to confession because there is no progress. On the other hand when you yearn to be better, when you are extremely anxious about your progress, it is apparent that you do not really want God. You do not as much want His mercy as your own perfection. Here lies your lack of faith. You go to confession so that eventually you will be so good that you will not need God who is Mercy Himself. You go to God for forgiveness so that you will not need His forgiveness any more, so that you can go on without Him, even though He always wants to forgive you, to forgive with joy.

How little faith we have in God's desire for continual forgiving. Among those who leave the confessional, there are always so few joyous faces. And yet after confession the world should be different for you, brighter, enlightened by faith in the merciful Lord.

In the Gospel, all the 'confessions' end with a feast: the Lord is a guest at the house of Zacchaeus and another time, the tax collector Matthew, the future Evangelist, invites Christ to a feast. Matthew also invites other tax collectors and sinners so that they could all celebrate with joy that he had received forgiveness. A feast was also prepared by the father of the Prodigal Son (cf. L. Evely, *Le chemin de joie*, 112). *The Gospel constantly links forgiveness with joy.*

Contrition is a decisive element in conversion. In the sacrament of reconciliation, you meet with Christ, who wants to forgive you and heal the wounds inflicted on you by your sin. However, if you do not show Jesus your wounds, then He cannot heal them.

If your contrition has no bounds, then the mercy of the Lord will also have no bounds. Think what your confessions are like. Contrition is an act of humility. Humility should increasingly grow within you and hence contrition should also continually grow. There is never enough contrition and never enough sorrow for the sins committed. The more you consider yourself a sinner and worse than others, the more you make room for grace and for your faith.

The sacrament of Penance should be an awaited sacrament, one should hunger for Christ present in it. This is a special time of our meeting with Christ. Love wants to be hungered for; otherwise it is wounded.

Those Who Guide You to the Sacrament of Conversion

One of the patrons of the sacrament of conversion is Zacchaeus. When we mention this unusual person, as a contrast, we are reminded of the rich young man in the Gospel. It must have been very difficult for the 'righteous' rich young man, to be contrite. He followed all the commandments of the Decalogue, so why should he be contrite? But Jesus said that for such a person it would be very difficult to enter the kingdom of heaven. He did not see within himself the greatest evil, the fact that he was so attached to riches and position that he did not choose God completely. He felt that since he followed the Decalogue then he was 'all right' before God. We don't know what happened to him later, but the evident pain felt by Jesus after he left, indicates just how bad his spiritual state was.

Next to the 'righteous' young man, the Gospel shows us an extreme case, a scoundrel, Zacchaeus. These sharp descriptions can be used because Zacchaeus, the chief of tax collectors, which meant he was chief of the collaborationists and thieves, was really a person worthy of pity in his own opinion and that of others around him. When this great sinner saw the merciful look of Jesus, something touched him inside and then his unusual reaction ensued: "Behold, Lord, the half of my goods I give to the poor; and if I have defrauded anyone of anything, I restore it four fold" (*Lk* 19:8). Who among us would be able to give up half of his possessions to the poor and make amends for wrongs four times over? There is in this incident the folly of generosity of a contrite sinner who discovers that he is loved. *Zacchaeus was truly overcome with astonishment and happiness.*

Jesus turned to the 'righteous' young man with the encouragement to give up his riches, but He said nothing to Zacchaeus; he did this on his own, without encouragement. We have, therefore, the contrast between a 'righteous' man who did not answer the 'look of mercy' and walked away saddened and the ringleader of thieves who turned out to be so sensitive to God's love.

The side candelabras found in many Polish churches are called 'zacheuszki' in Polish from the name Zacchaeus. The symbolism is profound. The 'zacheuszki' remind us of the unusual incident in which Jesus did not go for a meal with somebody 'righteous' such as the rich young man. Instead he said to the ringleader of thieves: "Zacchaeus, make haste and come down; for I must stay at your house today" (*Lk* 19:5). Coming to someone's house in those days meant entering into a kind of spiritual communion. This was not an ordinary visit for a meal or party. It was not only to eat something but also to enter into a special, intimate relationship. Jesus chose Zacchaeus to enter into this personal communion with him. Coming to his house, the house of presumably the most notorious thief in Jericho, He consecrated it just by His presence. Because of this, the house of Zacchaeus became almost a temple and sanctuary.

Maybe sometimes we feel like saying to Jesus: "Lord Jesus, what poor taste You have if You chose the home and heart of a thief as Your sanctuary." *But that is the way God is – to the point of folly in His love for man*.

Jesus came to Zacchaeus to bring redemption to his home. Bringing redemption to his home meant bringing it not only to Zacchaeus himself and his family but also to all of those similar to Zacchaeus, tax collectors and sinners, who came to him and sat with him at his table. Jesus came to enter into a communion with them, to receive them into the temple which He consecrated. *Zacchaeus' heart became God's sanctuary, for it was truly contrite*. Only from the heart of the contrite can Jesus make his true sanctuary.

The good thief is also the patron of the sacrament of reconciliation. His 'confession' took place on the cross. There he admitted his guilt: "And indeed, we have been condemned justly, for the sentence we have received corresponds to our crimes [...]" (*Lk* 23:41). What was happening within his soul remains a mystery to us. Only by the results can we try to assume a unique miracle of grace. This man must have been very contrite because with certainty he considered himself as being the worst. According to public opinion he was a criminal and a disgraced person since his crucifixion meant also being deprived of all rights. This criminal was dying by torture in public view and accepted this with his statement: "We suffer justly". It is as if he were saying: "Yes, this should happen to me, I deserve this". Somehow he must have then perceived the depth of his sinfulness and must have brought himself to be profoundly contrite. It is certain that his attitude of contrition and deep humility made his heart ready to accept God's gift of faith. How great must have been his faith if in the dying Jesus next to him, beaten, spat upon and still jeered at, he recognised the King: "Jesus, remember me when you come into your kingdom" (*Lk*23:42). It is so difficult for us to be converted because there is too little contrition in our hearts. If there is so little contrition then our faith is very shallow.

To Be Converted Towards Radicalism

The process of your conversion should lead you to Evangelical radicalism, the radicalism of faith to which God calls you through the words in the Book of Revelation of St John: "I wish you were either cold or hot. So, because you are lukewarm, neither hot nor cold, I will spit you out of my mouth" (*Rev* 3:15-16).

St John of the Cross stresses the importance of radicalism using an image of two tethered birds (cf. *The Assent of Mount Carmel*, Book One, Chapter 11,4 in: *The Collected works of St John of the Cross*, Washington D.C., 1991). One of them is tied by a cord and the other by a thin thread. In the end their situation is similar since both birds are tethered. The situation will change only when there will be no ties.

The opposite of radicalism is compromise, compromise in desires, in attitude, in prayer. God is a maximalist. He wants to give you everything, but you keep wanting too little and asking for too little. You still do not seek that which is most important, that which would be a realisation of your purpose in life, that Christ could be able to live fully and reign within you.

Do you know how much you tie God's hands when you ask for a little and are content with a compromise? In our life, everything should be directed toward one goal, *so that Christ can grow and reach His full dimension within us*. Everything should work toward this. That is why God requires radicalism in our petitions as well. God may not answer them since we ask for 'too little'. The fulfilment of our petitions for a place to live, good health and work may make us think that we do not need God any more. If this would not help us to follow the Lord to the end, then God may not want to answer such prayers. In His folly, God wants to give you everything. He wants to give you the kingdom, but you, wanting so little, make it impossible for Him.

Seek first, that is primarily, the kingdom of God and His righteousness, and everything else will be given you (cf. *Mt* 6:33). Someone once said that if you do not primarily seek the kingdom of God, then everything else will be taken from you. Every one of your problems and every difficulty is ultimately a call from God for you to desire more, infinitely more. You should seek above all else the kingdom of God, since then all else will be given to you. It is a call from God for your conversion, for your faith.

Marie spoke about the radicalism of her sister St Thérèse of the Child Jesus: "[...] you are possessed by God [...]" (*Letter to Thérèse from Marie*, September 17th 1896). Possessed, means the desire to give everything to the Lord. Try to follow her example, by desiring to give everything, increasingly more, so that Evangelical radicalism is embraced by your will, so that you too can become 'possessed' by God. Like St Thérèse you can then say, "I chose everything that You want" (*Manuscrits autobiographiques*). On the day of her death, in the evening of September 30th 1897, she said:

"Never would I have believed it was possible to suffer so much! Never! Never! I cannot explain this except by the ardent desires I have had to save souls", (*The Yellow Notebook*, September 30th 1897). St Thérèse suffered for you also, so that you too could be 'possessed' by God as she was, so that you too could live an Evangelical radicalism as she did.

St Ambrose emphasises that God does not look so much at what we offer to Him as gifts, but more at what we reserve for ourselves. God is a jealous God. He loves you to the end and wants you to open yourself up fully for His gifts so that He can bestow everything on you.

The meeting of Jesus with the rich young man is mentioned three times in the Gospel of St Matthew, St Mark and St Luke. This was really an unusual meeting: "As he was setting out on a journey, a man ran up, knelt down before him 'Good teacher, what must I do to inherit eternal life?' (*Mk* 10:17). Jesus answered him, 'If you wish to enter into life, keep the commandments. [...] You shall not kill. You shall not commit adultery. You shall not steal. You shall not bear false witness. Honour your father and your mother. And you shall love your neighbour as yourself'. The young man said to him (*Mt* 19:17-20), 'Teacher, all of these I have observed from my youth'. Jesus looking at him, loved him and said to him, 'You are lacking one thing. Go sell what you have and give to the poor and you will have treasure in heaven; then come follow me.' At that statement his face fell, and he went away sad, for he had many possessions'" (*Mk* 10:20-22).

Further describing this scene, St Luke goes on to tell us something unusual and surprising: "Jesus looked at him [now sad] and said, 'How hard it is for those who have wealth to enter the kingdom of God!'" (*Lk* 18:24). The disciples were astonished by these words. We would also be astonished. He had kept all the commandments. Jesus, however, "looked at him" and said how difficult it is for a man like him to enter the kingdom of God. This text is shocking. Jesus repeated this to the Apostles saying: "'Children' as if knowing how difficult this was for them: 'how hard it is for those who trust in riches to enter the kingdom of God! It is easier for a camel to go through the eye of a needle than for a rich man to enter the kingdom of God'. And they were exceedingly astonished, and said to him: 'Then who can be saved?'" (*Mk* 10:24-26). It appears from this that it is not enough to keep God's commandments, that *Christ's call to folly, which means to Evangelical radicalism, is our obligation.* We must, therefore, continually be converted towards this kind of radicalism. St Teresa of Avila, commenting on this text said that the rich young man lacked a seed of folly. He was, as St Luke writes, an official. He had therefore some important position. Thus, he would have had to give up many things, in fact everything. In his situation it would be a folly. He would have had to accept that people would say that he had lost his mind, for to give everything up is not that simple. Jesus says, however, that only he who gives up everything for God will enter the kingdom of heaven. It is not enough to love your neighbour as yourself. After all, the rich young man had followed all the commandments.

All of us are called to folly. Without that seed of folly we cannot follow the Lord to the end. Sooner or later we will have to leave everything and detach ourselves from everything. It will be most difficult to leave everything at the end when we are dying. Then we will have to do this but with great pain, and the Lord wants to save us from this pain. He would like us to leave all our riches now but not necessarily in the literal sense. It seems astonishing that the Lord demands so much of us, but this God's demand, comes from His desire for our freedom and for our own good. Evangelical folly depends on the fact that *we give up everything that is ours for God and He in turn gives us everything that is His. We give up our paltry everything and He gives us His wonderful everything, His Godly everything.* Let us learn from Mary, who is the example for us. She truly gave up everything to the Lord and followed Him to the end; the Mother of our abandonment to God, the Mother of our radicalism.

Chapter 2

A Pinch of Humour Amidst Faith

God is infinite mercy. He forgave David his adultery and murder, He forgave the greedy tax collector who was a traitor and He forgave the criminal on the cross. But there is, however, something that makes it impossible for God's mercy to be poured out and something that God detests within you – that is your unwavering, absolute seriousness; that you believe that you are someone important. Seeing this, it is as though God makes a gesture of spreading his hands out in helplessness. God finds your feeling of importance funny and absurd. "He who is enthroned in heaven laughs" (*Ps* 2:4). If you look at yourself *in the light of faith* then you will see that *all of your pretence of absolute seriousness and esteem are truly funny.*

The feeling of self-importance is opposed to a large degree by the 'virtue' of humour. It turns out to be very useful for the growth of our faith which is seeing the world in the proper light and with the correct sense of proportion. Humour is seeing the world on the axis of absurdity and nonsense. We have a patron of humour – St Thomas More. We also have a wealth of literature on this subject by authors such as G.K. Chesterton, C.S. Lewis, B. Marshal, F. Sheed and others. They write about the value of comedy, about humour used as a religious remedy benefiting faith, and about the 'theology' of humour.

Jansenism as a Great Threat to Faith

The heresy of Jansenism became a great threat to faith in the 16th century. Through Original Sin, as taught by Cornelius Jansen of Louvain, human nature was completely destroyed and covetousness was dominant. God granted His graces only to the chosen ones, and the others were destined for eternal damnation. This pessimistic outlook on human nature was coupled with the belief that Christ died not for all mankind, but only for the chosen ones.

Jansenism set unattainable requirements for receiving Holy Communion which the average Christian did not have. Complete freedom from sin, even venial sins, and absolutely pure love of God were required. The Eucharist became a payment for virtue and not the nourishment which strengthens faith and love. In the churches dominated by Jansenism, there was the mood of sadness, grimness and terror. Man began to fear God. Only rarely would he be brave enough to receive the Eucharist.

The Cistercian abbey in Port Royal became the centre of Jansenism. The "Rosary to the Most Blessed Sacrament", written by one of the nuns there, which emphasises everything that separates God from man, is a testimony to the prevailing mood. God was not presented as a merciful and loving Father, but as an absolute, inaccessible, strict and ruthless Lord. According to Jansenistic views, a Christian is a repentant sinner; therefore he cannot allow himself to experience joy. His life should be dominated by the sadness which comes from remembering his own sins. Blaise Pascal's sister, the director of the Girls boarding house in Port Royal, forbade laughter in the regulations for her pupils; even smiles were discouraged.

Jansenism was condemned several times by the Apostolic See, but its effects were still experienced by St Thérèse of Lisieux, who had to obtain special permission from her superior to receive Holy Communion more often. Another effect of Jansenism that appears often in a modern Christians' life is the fear of God, seeing Him only as the fair Judge. But Christian faith most fully expresses itself in the joy of discovering the personal love of God, which you can depend on and to which you can entrust yourself. Faith experienced in this way eradicates the attitude of dramatic fatalism toward one's own evil, which our contrition can change into a 'happy fault'. Christian joy flowing from faith is like a radiation of God's love. It is faith that tells you to smile at God, to be joyful in His love. Then you should look

at yourself, whom you take much too seriously, from a certain distance and with a humorous perspective. The 'virtue'
of humour lets you defeat the poison of sadness, with which
Satan tries to permeate your soul. This virtue of humour
causes you to cease worrying about yourself and allows you
to live a life of joy flowing from faith.

Humour as an 'Exorcism'

The 'virtue' of humour, which is seeing the absurd in the
world, is a religious remedy which may have the *value of
an exorcism*. When you are resisting a wave of temptations, a wave of persistent thoughts which can tire you, do
not fight with Satan, for he is stronger than you, but try to
deride him and scoff at him. Use this 'exorcism', which is
a religious sense of humour, by making fun of Satan. You
can then repel his attack in the most effective way. *A ridiculed Satan is most forcefully struck*, since he is deadly
serious, and very afraid of ridicule, and is therefore com-
pelled to leave you.

The Christian sense of humour will also help you fight
another enemy: your own 'self'. This is also an idol, which is
deadly serious, untouchable and absolute. It cannot be
touched or ridiculed; it cannot be offended or criticised.
Using humour to fight this idol becomes a religious remedy
and an act of faith when you look at yourself and try to see
that 'self' in the appropriate light: In reality, I am truly such
a small 'nothing'. Why then do I make myself the centre of
the universe? Why do I believe that my concerns are the
most important? Why do I suffer for my defeats and troubles so much, and why am I so deadly serious? It would
suffice to look at everything with a little bit of friendly scoff,
to see what I am so worried about, what I fear and what
I care about is really silly compared to the one important
reality which is God.

*Christian humour is a remedy by which the idol of
your 'self' is dethroned*. When you see the humour in

a situation in which your 'self' ascends to the throne, then, at least for a while, this situation is ridiculed and becomes harmless to you. Your vanity and pride become unmasked; that which pretended to be great or to be the threat arousing fear in you is ridiculed and unmasked. In this way, the religious remedy of humour also has the significant role of preserving your psychological balance.

Ashes and Dust

Humour is a 'religious remedy' by which you can tell yourself, "Look how absurd I am, I worry about trifles, I have so many troubles, I am ruining my health. But, in reality everything is like ashes, like rubbish and finally may prove to be worthless. Try to look at your life in the light of faith; *try to joke about yourself.* This may be difficult because the 'virtue' of humour sometimes requires heroism. Nevertheless it enables you to attain the proper proportion between the two realities: God and yourself. In this way, the virtue of humour cleanses your faith of egoism and strengthens it. It will show you with great clarity that only God is really important in your life. That is why you should not make yourself the centre of the universe. *Perceive yourself as* a small grain of sand, as St Thérèse spoke of herself, *a small 'nothing',* which should not be too much cared for or troubled or worried about: "Pray," asked the Saint, "that the *grain of sand* become an *atom* seen only by the eyes of Jesus!" (*Letter from Thérèse to Sister Agnes,* January 6th 1889).

The Christian sense of humour will free you from yourself. It will allow you to re-evaluate every value in the light of faith, and to acknowledge that everything that happens around you is really ridiculously insignificant – everything except God. It will allow you to unmask those things which only seem to be values. In comparison with the value which is God, everything in the end is *ashes and dust* – your work, your plans and your troubles, politics and that which happens all around you. It is in this spirit that we began Lent with the liturgy of Ash Wednesday, when the priest places ashes on your head and says that from dust you have arisen and into dust you shall return. Dust is something ridiculously insignificant. Not only are you dust, but also all that you really care for and all you are attached to, as well as all that you fear. Thanks to the 'virtue' of humour, you will open yourself more fully to God. There will be more room for Him because you are able to see everything else in its proper perspective – as ashes and dust. It means that you are able to set all this on the axis of absurdity.

With a perspective such as this we are able to see, for example, the conversion of St Francis of Assisi. When he threw everything at the feet of his father in order to follow the voice of God, suddenly he was free. It was as if the whole world turned upside down: "Whoever has seen the whole world hanging by a thread of God's Mercy, has really seen the truth. [...] Whoever has had the vision of his home town turned upside down, has seen it the way it should be seen [...] The man that has seen the hierarchy turned upside down will always have a slight smile towards its prerogatives" (G. K. Chesterton, *Saint Francis of Assisi*, ch. 5).
Assisi was the country and homeland of St Francis of Assisi. It was a feudal town surrounded by a moat, walls and towers. Society in Assisi at that time was a 'noble' pyramid made up of several social groups each subordinate to the other. There were the serious city elders, the serious noblemen, the burghers and the serfs. And suddenly this world was turned upside down and in the eyes of Francis it became something ridiculously insignificant. It would take only one push for Assisi's world of important city elders, lords and noblemen to crack and collapse. All of this, seen by Francis on the axis of the absurd, became like ashes and dust. In the face of God, human strength became ridiculous and unimportant. Francis understood that there is only one important, serious reality worth living for, that is God and His will. It is God's will that one must never laugh at; it should be loved. One should, as a child, trustfully hold onto that which alone is important.

At the basis of most sins lies steadfast importance and absolute gravity. *You sin because you are so very important*. Casting aside this importance through Christian humour, writes Walter Kasper, makes us capable of: "a serene and truly human existence" (comp. *Einführung in den Glauben*, ch. 7). Humour points out the drollness of our pretending to be important. The lack of humour and the accompanying irritability is one of the most important accusations levelled at modern Christians.

The Pharisees were people who where deadly serious. They were so very certain of their gravity and importance. At the same time they were so attached to their vision of the world and God, that they reacted aggressively to accusations. Pharisaism is the opposite of simplicity. Simplicity includes freedom which flows from living in the truth and from seeing oneself in truth. Pharisaism at the same time is a contradiction to the attitude of an Evangelical child who, acknowledging his own weakness, is free of the feeling of importance. It should be remembered that a sin against the Holy Spirit is one, where among other things, a person does not want to accept the truth about himself and does not acknowledge his own weakness.

Supernatural humour allows us to discover the true proportion between human and Godly realities. It allows us to gain greater distance, detachment and greater freedom. *Being distanced* from occurrences and from ourselves, achieved *thanks to a sense of humour, enables us live the Gospel more fully*. It allows for change in priorities in our own life and our own concerns stop being the most important. It allows us to avoid being extremely absorbed, to avoid excessive problems and inundation of work, in order to hear Christ's calling that there is need of only one thing (cf. *Lk* 10:42). Owing to the 'virtue' of humour, failures and losses do not become life's tragedies. Faith supported by humour can carry you even to the summits of detachment. Evangelical freedom is exemplified by St Paul's principle of using the world in such a way as not to use it: "From now on, let those having wives act as not having them, those weeping as not weeping, those rejoicing as not rejoicing, those buying as not owning, those using the world as not using it fully" (*1 Co* 7:29-31). Saint John of the Cross encourages: "Strive so that all things are nothing to you and you nothing to them" (*Advice and Guidelines* – Puntos de amor).

St Thérèse of the Child Jesus spoke of herself as a grain of sand, a small 'nothing'. This is how her childlike attitude was expressed; it contains none of the grave seriousness which lies at the base of many of our sins. Most of our sins toward those who are close to us, come about from the fact that we became insulted and hurt over nothing. In that which concerns us, we are often oversensitive and touchy. All of those sensitive, oversensitive and touchy people need a sense of humour, which liberates and brings freedom from their own selves. For people overly sensitive about themselves even the smallest detail grows to huge proportions. If we knew how to react with a sense of humour to various conflicts, arguments and misunderstandings and if we allowed ourselves to be laughed at a little, how much would our humility, faith and love grow within us. *In the light of faith, there is, however, only one important reality that must never be laughed at – God.*

Try to take yourself and that which surrounds you a little less seriously and look at all of it more in the light of faith. You will then see how often that which touches you deeply is fitting to be laughed or joked about. *Try to laugh to yourself and at yourself.* Try to imitate God who must surely have a unique sense of humour. It is sufficient to consider that He chose you as his partner in the great work that He does. Is this not an expression of His unique sense of humour?

The Saint with Humour

The 'virtue' of humour in the saints reached such a degree of heroism that it radiated even in the face of great suffering or death. St Thomas More, a saintly man, but still only a man, experienced psychophysical fears that arose in him just as we experience them. No one is free from fears; even our Saviour experienced them. St Thomas most certainly feared the quartering and torture that he was told he would suffer. Later the sentence of torture was changed to beheading.

On the day of the execution Sir Thomas More changed into his best clothes and the Lieutenant seeing this, demanded that he dress down. Finally, Sir Thomas had to do this. He was then brought out of the Tower and led to the place of execution. Before he walked onto the scaffold, the mood was very sombre and difficult to endure. A religious remedy of humour was needed. Thomas More then said to the officer in charge of the execution who was also deadly serious: "I pray you, Mr Lieutenant, see me safely up, and as for my coming down let me shift for myself" (W.Roper & N.Harpsfield, *Lives of Saint Thomas More*, London, New York 1963, p.50). This quip is full of humour in the face of his own death.

King Henry VIII forbade him to speak – it is obvious how a person such as this can affect the people, a person whose sense of humour does not abandon him even in the face of death. What power this is! Even Satan fears a person with a true sense of religious humour, let alone Henry VIII. There was, therefore, no speech. The prisoner knelt, and after saying a prayer turned to the executioner and with a cheerful expression said to him, "Pluck up thy spirits, man, and be not afraid to do thine office. My neck is very short. Take heed, therefore, thou strike not awry thus saving thine honour" (W.Roper & N.Harpsfield, *Lives of Saint Thomas More*, p.50). Those were the last words of Thomas More, he was able to laugh at himself; put himself, his concerns and even his own death on the axis of the absurd. For in the face of God, the one reality for whom it is worth living, even our own death is unimportant. He truly must have had the soul of a child, holding his Father's hand very tightly in order to be able to joke in the face of his own death. This was done by one who had often prayed for a Christian sense of humour.

Chapter 3

Trials of Faith

In order for faith to become strong, it must be tried. It must go through a crucible of experiences, through many trials and storms. A shallow faith dependent solely on education, feelings and certain habits, collapses in the face of difficulties. In trials of faith, God wants a person who believes, to become stripped of that which is not faith, but is only a support of faith. God wants a person to be stripped of that which is not true adherence to Christ, is not reliance on Him and is not entrusting oneself to Him.

True faith is free from all natural supports such as understanding, feelings, and intellectual or imaginative experiences. True faith is dependent solely on Him and on His word. God does not accept the situation in which you base your faith on your actions, your feelings or your experiences. Therefore, He allows trials of faith which differ depending on what, besides God, you place your faith in. If you rely on your natural understanding, all clearness of your reason must vanish. At a certain point that which you have believed in, starts to make no sense. If you have placed your faith in certain people, laymen or clergymen and their actions, then even this at a certain point must sway or collapse. If you have relied your faith on feelings, on the satisfaction and joy experienced in prayer or religious practices, then you must not be surprised when a time comes of spiritual dryness and an aversion to those practices. You have to go through this painful cleansing in order to gain a pure, true faith and eventually true contemplation.

Hungry for God

God, placing man in difficult situations, provokes him into performing acts of faith. These situations, by making us realise our powerlessness, can deepen our yearning for God. God does not want to come to us uninvited. *Love wants to be looked for*; otherwise, love is pushed away. In this sense, *faith looks for God to come*. The intensity of looking for God to come, indicates the greatness of faith in His power and His love. We can never look enough for God to come. It intensifies due to your attempts to look for Him to come. However, this occurs primarily due to God's grace, which causes your yearning for Him, to grow and deepen within you. God has His ways to enliven your looking for Him and for His graces that follow.

There are two specific categories of these ways of God. First, He can stir the desire within our hearts for His coming, for example, through some creative anxiety or great need. Faith will then be expressed by a need for God. The growth of faith will be indicated by your *increasingly intensive looking for God to come and your hungering for Him.* At other times, He may allow or cause you to go through difficult *trials of faith* when you will not be able to cope with your problems by yourself. These could be moral problems, for example, sins that you commit, family problems such as a crumbling marriage, or a problem with a son who gets drunk, who is living with someone outside of marriage or is an unbeliever. These trials can be problems with health which could suddenly fail you or someone close to you. The experience of not being able to cope with something and the feeling of loss can cause you to have the desire to look for His coming. This is a chance for the growth and the deepening of your faith. All of these difficulties and problems, which God allows or causes to come into your life are meant to awaken in you the hunger for God; they are trials of faith. Looking at all of this in the light of faith, you will come to know the so-called spirituality of events which says that every event is God's passing by. Certain experiences of God's passing by are orientated towards awakening in you the desire for His presence, His help and His redemptive intervention. The more you feel ill, the more you feel the need for a doctor. The more you feel helpless and crushed by various difficulties, the greater the desire within you for the coming of Him, who can help you, who imparts His redemptive grace to all of your problems and who can save you. All you need to do is to believe that He wants to give you everything you need, to believe in His might and boundless love.

When God wants you to reach the depths of faith, He can give you very difficult trials; He can take much away from you and even strip you of many supports. God may want you to become uprooted so that, not having any human se-curities, you can look for redemptive help to come from Him alone.

The Faith of Abraham

Abraham the father of our faith, is the patron of our look-ing for God to come. How did God make Abraham look for Him to come? God uprooted him.

God's first call, according to the Bible, was: "Go forth from the land of your kinsfolk and from your father's house to a land that I will show you" (*Gen* 12:1). So Abraham, rooted in his native Haran, not far from Ur in the Chaldeans, obeyed God. And when he departed from his native land and became stripped of every support, he had no choice but to listen intently to the Word of God. In this way, his faith grew, for Abraham became increasingly more reliant on the will of God, and asked *what God expected from him*. And in this way, a new phenomenon appears in the history of mankind; a phenomenon of Christian faith resulting from the call of God to a person and from the existential naked-ness of man. Abraham's faith and self-entrustment to God is born from being uprooted and from the uncertainty expe-rienced by him. In Abraham, a man of faith is born and grows in his maturity. Our birth into faith will not be easy, either. It will also be a result of trials and difficulties, a result of our nakedness, of threatening situations and when there is nothing to rely on.

God is a God of promises and blessings. Abraham received the promise of a land, descendants and a special blessing from God. It was not, however, a clear promise but one clouded with a certain darkness. God says: "Go forth [...] to a land that I will show you", but Abraham had never seen this land, because a free land or one that was waiting for his arrival did not exist. Abraham did not know how this promise from God would be fulfilled, but he *entrusted this to his Lord*. Such was the greatness of faith in Abraham. The promise of descendants was also unclear, for he was an old man. From a human point of view, this seemed rather unlikely. Abraham had to believe in something which in human terms would seem impossible.

The more God's promise seems unlikely, the more God demands and expects from us; but the greater will be the merit of our trusting response. The promise made to Abraham was so improbable, that he had to believe that God is a God of impossible and improbable things. For Abraham, achieving this belief, would be a long, continuous process of growing in faith. When he reached the promised land, it was not his to keep. He would always be a stranger. However, the greatest deepening of his faith came under more dramatic conditions. God demanded of him the sacrifice of his son, which is the sacrifice of someone who is most dear to him. From a human point of view, his son is his greatest treasure and that which is of greatest value to him. This situation was incredibly difficult. Abraham must have, therefore, expected that God would somehow resolve this terrifying situation caused by His demand. Abraham had to decide to trust boundlessly. The demand God made of Abraham struck at his fatherly feelings, at his greatest love for his only and beloved son. At the same time God struck Abraham, at the very foundation of the faith he had held until then. Abraham had believed that many descendants would come from his son. What God demanded of him might have seemed all the more absurd. The one from whom so many promised descendants were to be born, is now to be killed. God demanded so much from Abraham because He wanted to grant him something special; *He wanted to raise his trust to the peak.* Abraham's trial of faith was not really a trial; God already knew how Abraham would react. This trial provoked him to make a decision so that in darkness, he would trust in God in a special way. In this way *he moved forward towards Him in his pilgrimage of faith.* The most difficult situations are of particular advantage since they demand crucial decisions. *Faith develops through decisions* by which man devotes himself to God through the "obedience of faith" (cf. *Qo* 5).

You will also undergo a trial like that of Abraham, because God, in loving you, will sometimes place you in a difficult situation. He will allow or cause something to be a great burden for you and extremely difficult to bear. You will be unable to cope with it. All this, so that you will begin to look for Him to come, and that you will desire Him. He will make it impossible for you to remain in a state of religious stagnation. The trial of faith, that you will then encounter, will force your faith to be polarised. Either you will not answer God's desire and you will begin to retreat in your faith, or as Abraham, you will decide to entrust yourself to Him in the darkness of faith. Then your faith, your hunger for Christ and His Redemption and your hunger for grace, will grow in you. To the extent of this hunger will the Holy Spirit be able to descend into your heart.

Trials of Faith in the Life of Mary

The Church begins the calendar year with the day dedicated to the Blessed Mother. On January the first, we are shown the figure of her, who "who advanced in her pilgrimage of faith" (*LG* 58). In Mary's life, the blessing stated to her by Elizabeth "Blessed are you who believed" (*Lk* 1:45) was brought about every day. The Church, therefore, sees Mary as the most complete example for our faith.

Mary goes before us, leading the way in the 'pilgrimage of faith', as if she were anticipating our steps. Mary is near us on our road to faith. According to conciliar thought, the Blessed Mother is pre-eminent and wholly unique in the Church (*LG* 53), while at the same time she is closest to us. It could be said that we hurt the Blessed Mother when we speak only of her eminence and elevation and by so doing we create a distance between her and us. Too much is said about her distinctiveness and too little about the fact that *she is our way, and that this way is christocentric*. Mary is our way in the sense that she goes before us and shows us the way of faith, as she has already experienced everything which could happen to us. Looking at her life, we should find answers to our problems.

When we speak only about the nobleness and exaltation of the Blessed Mother, we treat her the way hagiographers often treated the saints. Someone once said that the saints suffered most not at the hands of their persecutors but at the hands of hagiographers who, by removing their simple human characteristic from their biographies, made them up to be sugary lifeless figures. It is not enough to honour Mary, to adore her and place crowns on her head. These are so called 'rich means' which she never used in her life. To love Mary means to imitate her and follow her, for she is the one that goes before us, the one that is an example for our faith.

If we are surprised that God foils our plans and leads us down a different road from the one we imagined, let us recall that it was the same in the life of the Blessed Mother. Mary also thought of her sanctity, her road, her mission differently. The one who gave up her motherhood was called to an exceptional and unique motherhood. This call foiled all of her plans. Mary, by answering the Annunciation with her "yes", did not fully realise what she was agreeing to. This, however, did not diminish the value of her consent which she later confirmed with her continual "yes" throughout her life. God so loved Mary that He chose this very rigorous way of treating her. We know that this is the way He treats His friends. This is the best method for allowing the shaping of a person in the image of the Son of God.

Let us look at the way God formed Mary's faith, during the 'hurricanes' that went through her life and the difficulty of her trials. Shortly after Mary's first 'fiat', when it was announced to her that she would conceive and bear the Son of God, it turned out that St Joseph knew nothing about this. This was the first tragedy for both of these people. Mary and Joseph did not know what to do and they suffered greatly because of this. It must have been a shock to Joseph when he realised that Mary was with child and it was also a torment for her. Surely, it would not have been difficult for God to explain the situation to Joseph. During this time, Mary must have been continually asking herself, "What shall I do?" This was a difficult time full of darkness for her.

Faith does not remove darkness; it does just the opposite, it requires it. This truth reveals the meaning of faith. The Blessed Mother, living in faith, lived in great darkness and was therefore tested in her faith in a sometimes exceptionally hard manner. The birth of Jesus in Bethlehem was a trial of this kind. The time and place of childbirth is for every mother a sensitive issue. A mother wants to give birth in a worthy place, under human conditions – this is her basic right. Did not Mary long for this? However, this was not granted to her. If Jesus had to be born in Bethlehem, would it not have been easier for Mary if Joseph had learned about this in advance? He was being given instructions in his sleep anyway, so he could have also received the instruction 'Go to Bethlehem for that is where the Child will be born'. Meanwhile, God decided to arrange things in a different way. The Child was born in Bethlehem due to the unusual circumstance of a census. As a result of this situation, Jesus was born under such poor conditions, without any securities. Because of the crowds of newcomers, it was hard to find any room. It would have been so easy then to succumb to the temptation of doubt and fear. And in the difficult situation of this trial of faith, the Child was to be born. The angel appeared to Mary only during the Annunciation. After that there were no further instructions, no further messages or mission. During the birth of Jesus, the angels appeared only to the shepherds tending their flocks, but not to Mary. Soon after, along with the coming of the Three Wise Men, the next 'earthquake' came the persecution by Herod. A difficult trial of faith when questions such as these may arise: Why is God silent? Why does He not intervene to defend His Son? Why does He appear powerless in the face of Herod's tyranny? And why is there the necessity to escape to an unknown land where there is no human support?

The next trial of faith which proved to be very difficult, arose when the young Jesus remained in the temple, without previously telling His parents about it. The Gospel says that they did not understand the words He spoke to them when they found Him; Mary only kept them in her heart. Thus, darkness continued in her life. Why did Jesus not want to explain anything to her? She, *the Mother of God, had to learn the correct way to interpret events*. She had to learn the spirituality of events. God did not make anything easier for her; everything in her life was always so very difficult.

The "yes" during the Annunciation seems joyous and easy compared to the last "yes" spoken under the Cross. A person on a high level in his spiritual life is usually ready to sacrifice his own self. It is much more difficult to agree to the suffering of those close to us, the ones we love very much. Mary, standing at the Cross, gave a double "yes", *let it so happen to us; to Him and to me*. If my beloved Son is to suffer and be tortured, then let it be so. Agreeing to this was the supreme sacrifice. This 'fiat' of Mary's at the Cross caused her to become the Mother of the Church, and Mother of us all. *That most difficult "yes" was the source of Mary's spiritual motherhood*. If you are very upset or depressed by something, think that you are then close to Mary whose life was so very difficult. God loved Mary in a special, exceptional way, but in her life there was so much suffering. Such is the way that God treats His friends.

It is a special form of God's love and trust to us, when He wants us not to expect Him to show us His feelings, so that He is free to act. We can imagine an ideal marriage in a situation where the husband is very busy with some kind of work. The wife, who loves him, does not want to bother him with anything. She herself finds the materials he needs, trying to help him as best she can. She thinks only of him. This is that ideal love when a person thinking about someone else, diminishes himself, not seeking any attention for himself. This is an unusually difficult love. This is the kind of love Christ demanded of His mother.

This is portrayed in the Evangelical scene about the meeting which was to take place between Jesus and Mary and His closest family. He was told: "Your mother and your brothers are standing outside, asking to speak with you" (*Mt* 12:47). Jesus then treated His mother the way He could treat only the person He loved very much, the one He had the utmost trust in. He spoke as if He were refusing her: "Who is my mother? Who are my brothers? (*Mt* 12:48). It may have seemed that Christ was very brusque toward his mother, but these were her trials of faith, trials of her total devotion to God. For Mary, this harsh treatment was the expression of the highest trust shown toward her by her Son. Mary knew that Jesus was counting on her and she did not expect to be particularly honoured by Him. Mary never stood in the way of Jesus' apostolic mission, and this was the evidence of her greatest, selfless love for her Son. If He sometimes appears harsh to you it means that He loves you very much and trusts that you will not disappoint Him and leave. Christ continually stripped His mother of her supports and she continued to say "yes" to Him. She became increasingly like the godly example of her Son.

Can this life be described as a very difficult one?
– Yes and no. This ambivalence occurs because these *events of being stripped of supports can become joy and happiness* for a person who loves God and is united with Him. That is *because they are an opportunity to profess one's love for God and prove loyalty and faith in Him.*

Whenever it is hard or difficult for you and He remains silent, remember that this silence is just another form of His word, and His absence is just another form of His permanent overwhelming Presence. When it seems to us that Jesus is silent and absent, it is not really so. This is indicated by the words God told St Teresa of Avila: "When you thought that you were alone, I was nearest to you". When you feel very alone, when it is hard for you, when you are experiencing some kind of nakedness, He is closest to you. However, He does not give you signs because He wants you to trust in Him even more. *This kind of silence and this seeming absence is a risk for Him.* Some people then leave. At one time, a great deal of the people who were listening to Jesus, left, because they thought that Jesus was demanding too much of them. This leaving Jesus, caused by trials of faith, is continually repeated. Some come through the trials strengthened by their trust in God; others walk away from Him.

Mary's attitude in the face of such difficult trials of faith awakens our guilty conscience. In her life, all trials of faith ended with a deepening of her self-entrusting to God. Although she went through so many difficult experiences, she never failed God. There was no divergence in Mary between the ideal of a person and the realisation of this. God's ideal was brought about in her life so fully that she became God's masterpiece, the most perfect realisation of His plans. We, on the other hand, constantly create a dissonance between our faith and life, between our words and deeds, between our ideals and their realisation. As the result of trials of faith, we retreat or we may even leave. It is in this sense, that the example of Mary awakens our guilty conscience.

Mary, who serves as an example of trusting abandonment to God, could be called the Blessed Mother of Acceptance or, Mother of Abandonment to God, since she continually said to God: "Let it happen the way You want". The most important event in the history of the world happened in the darkness of the night in Gethsemane. This event was Christ's − "yes" spoken to His Father. The most important events in your life will occur when, just as Mary did, you choose the way of giving consent to God continually. Her consent stretched throughout her entire life. It should also be the same for you. Your life is comprised of continual 'annunciation's' understood as calls of grace and as trials of faith. Time is priceless because it is the presence of God. The current moment is a call directed to us. It is a trial of faith. It is God's question: "will you say 'yes' to me?" Our life in faith is brought down to this 'yes'. *The essence of Christianity is the continual saying to God: "Thy will be done"*. The Blessed Mother continually repeated these words to God. Can anyone love more than she did?

Mary was always full of grace, and at the same time she continually grew in grace. Through loyalty and trust, this special human soul became like a vessel, which despite always being full of grace, was able to continually receive more. Is this not a paradox? It was as if God continually expanded her heart, and every new trial of faith, every "yes" caused her to grow in grace. The Blessed Mother's life, ordinary and grey, was being sanctified with this continual *fiat*.

The distance between Mary and us is always brought about through our fault. It is we, who make her unreachable and distant. It is this very distance that accuses us of mediocrity, minimalism, compromise, and fear of responding to the grace completely. It is much easier to say that she was Immaculately Conceived, that she was the Mother of God, that she was exceptional and that I can not imitate her. But this is only an excuse and the setting up of obstacles to the impelling call of the grace to follow in her footsteps.

We could ask, why is it so important to Jesus that we follow in her footsteps, to go toward Him in Mary's way. One of the answers to this question is the radicalism of the Blessed Mother, the radicalism of a devotion to God which makes possible God's offering Himself to us. Jesus loved Mary in an unusual and exceptional way. He loved no other creature as He loved her, because she was able to give up everything to Him. She, who had chosen virginity, realised this not only in the sense of maintaining chastity in celibacy, but also in complete devotion out of love to God. That is what Mary's Evangelical virginity depended on.

Her evangelical virginity depended on her determined will to live in chastity in order to completely devote herself to God and live for Him.

Mary from the first moment of her existence, adhered to the Everlasting Word with all the strength of her will and love. And it is in this way that Mary realised the highest ideal of virginity in her life. Mary, through abandoning herself to God without reservation and in a perfect way, first became the Bride and then the Mother of the Word.

God offers Himself to the soul to the extent to which it devotes itself to Him. How great then, must the Word have offered itself to Mary, if she so totally became a gift for Him. *Mary's soul is a type of soul which Jesus so loved for Her total abandonment to God.* Jesus wants us to choose Mary's way because He wants us to fulfil our lives by having the type of soul He loves for its total devotion. His deep desire is to find souls similar to hers, souls who follow Him to the end, and to overwhelm them with the infinite wellspring of His love and His graces. The desire to find souls such as this is His 'hunger', which is never satisfied within Him. He calls you to go Mary's way, in order to reveal the greatness of His desires for you.

If you will imitate Mary and become increasingly like her, then Jesus will be able, to the extent of your devotion, to love you with the same love that He loved her. Mary appears to you as the type of soul fully devoted to God. Mary's example calls you to bring about the ideal of the radicalism of faith.

Storms in our Lives

An especially privileged time for the development of our faith is when we experience storms in our lives. The storm at sea described in the Gospel is a certain symbol for our situation. During difficult trials of faith, in the times of lesser or greater storms, it seems to us that Jesus has abandoned us, that He is not there.

There can be various storms: the storms of temptations, storms of scruples, storms of worrying about the future, about health, and about work, storms involving discord in marriage. In the face of a storm, two types of attitudes can be observed; fear, as in the case of the terrified Apostles, and peace, symbolised by the sleeping Jesus in the boat. Jesus is sleeping through a human tragedy, in a boat tossed by the waves, and in danger of being sunk at any moment. He must have been tired; but was it only His tiredness? Jesus slept in the Apostle's boat and they thought that everything was lost. This is where their panic, stress and terror came from, when they woke Jesus. During that storm, two attitudes were revealed. On the one hand, one could see the faces of the Apostles contorted in fear and on the other hand, the peaceful face of Jesus who was sleeping. Christ's attitude seemed so strange that the Apostles accused Him: "Teacher, do you not care that we are perishing?" (Mk 4:38).

Every storm has its purpose. It is God's passing by which will bring with it some great grace, primarily the grace of trust. During a storm, you should direct the eyes of your faith on the peaceful face of Christ. A "theology of God's sleep" could be discussed here. During our storms, God seems to be sleeping. The revelation of the Bible includes not only God's word, but also God's gestures. How very rich in context is this very gesture of Jesus' sleep during the dramatic moment of threat. Of course, this does not mean that when threatened with danger, one should do nothing. Quietism is contradictory to the teaching of the Church. Jesus does not reproach the Apostles that they tried to save the boat. He accused them of the lack of an attitude of faith, which caused them to succumb to the temptation of fear or even panic. It is with this gesture of sleep, that He wanted to tell them: "But I am with you, you should be calm, for nothing can happen to the boat that I am in".

116

The attitude of faith is simultaneously a prayer of faith. It is expressed by calm in the face of danger, by peace on a spiritual level, because we have no direct influence on our psychophysical level. There will be many anxieties that will tear us apart, but that is not important. What is important is that fear, which is aroused in our emotional and mental level, does not control our spiritual level. It is important that it does not cause a change in our attitude, our deeds, thoughts and desires. Our faith and belief in the fact that He is present here close to us, makes us calm in spite of our emotional state. His presence is a presence of eternal power and eternal love.

When the storms come into your life, internal or external, look at the peaceful face of Jesus. Then you will understand that you are not alone and that He, in every situation is saying, "this storm will pass; it has to pass".

During our storms and our trials of faith, we must also never forget about the continuous presence of Mary who is close to us, as the Mother of our abandonment to God. Let us ask her to allow us to share in her abandonment to God, that we stop trusting ourselves, things, and people and that we may perceive the continuous presence of her Son, who is close to us and who is our only security. We ask Mary that we, following her example, trust exclusively in the Lord: "Mother of Great Abandonment, I offer you myself without reservation, to the end".

Anxiety Arising from Lack of Faith

Trials of faith do not always strengthen faith or make it more dynamic. If you reject the stripping of yourself, which is connected with the trials, then you retreat from entrusting yourself to God. Your faith in the face of difficulties will start to collapse. Your life will be dominated by anxiety, haste and stress – symptoms of an immature faith or the lack of it, which negates the very life of faith.

In the face of trials of faith, which may be some kind of threat or difficulty, when you succumb to haste, anxiety and stress, you wound the love of Jesus. When you then take these difficult matters into your own hands and want to solve them on your own, *you simply count on yourself*, and then there is no room for faith. Faith is the reliance on His might and His boundless love. When you allow anxiety, haste or stress to overcome you, it is as though you were pushing Jesus aside and as though you were saying, "I cannot count on You now, I have to take this matter into my own hands".

Of course, you have to differentiate between the two levels in a person; the psychophysical level and the spiritual level. The psychophysical level of a person, the level of a person's feelings, is the first to be overcome by haste, anxiety and stress in the face of difficulties and threats. As long as that inner tension which pushes you to haste or anxiety remains in the psychophysical level, you do not hurt Jesus. However, you may allow that mentally difficult situation for you and all the anxiety or haste coming from it, to overcome your spiritual faculties, which are your thoughts and your will. This already reveals your unfaithfulness and lack of faith. It does not mean that you should remove fear, haste or anxiety from your psychophysical level, for often this is impossible. It does mean that there should be no panic in your attitude, which is determined and formed by your spiritual sphere so that peace flowing from faith can dominate there.

It is not easy to maintain an attitude of peace. Saints also had to struggle often with difficulties of this kind. For example, St Maximillian had stomach ulcers, which may suggest, that he must have experienced nervous tension. There was a time in his life when he actually ordered himself to be calm in the face of threats. Thus he had to fight for his faith.

The virtue of fortitude does not necessarily imply that we do not feel fear or anxiety on the psychophysical level. It does imply that we do not succumb to that fear. It means believing that we are never alone, that there is always Someone with us who loves us and upon whom everything is dependent. Difficult graces of trials of faith often involving suffering, should be accepted by us with the awareness of the closeness of Christ. We should accept them with the belief that He will be victorious, that after Good Friday, Resurrection Sunday will come. There should be an unshaken faith within us, that He who is peace, power, joy, and the Resurrection, is with us even more so during our trials and suffering.

Living by the present moment, sanctifying it as a moment of grace, is an expression of the dynamism of our faith and of our fight with the temptations of anxiety, haste, and stress: "Surrender yourself totally into the hands of the Merciful Providence, that is into the hands of the Immaculate, and be at peace", wrote St Maximillian to one of the brothers in the convent (K. Strzelecka, *Maksymilian Maria Kolbe*).

Live as if this were your last day. Tomorrow is uncertain, yesterday does not belong to you, only today is yours. God does not want you to look back because then, most often, you succumb to those temptations of anxiety, haste and stress. "No one who sets a hand to the plough and looks to what was left behind him is fit for the kingdom of God" (*Lk* 9:62).

Nor does God want you to worry about the future. In the Sermon on the Mount, Jesus clearly states: "Sufficient for a day is its own evil" (*Mt* 6:34). If you look back at the past or look to the future, you are not living the present moment; you lose the 'grace of the moment' which He wants to bestow upon you.

Living in the present moment can be imagined through a certain fictional scene, which is like a parable: Imagine that you are standing on a platform, with a long train passing by with many empty cars which you have to load with packages which are lying beside you. When you start looking at the cars that have passed, you may notice with fright the multitude of cars that have not been loaded (you are thinking about the past). Then you may look at the ones that are approaching you and again are frightened that there are still so many cars left to be loaded (you are thinking about the future). *In the meantime however, another car has passed by unloaded.* (You are letting the present moment and the graces connected with it slip by)

Anxieties that nag you about the past or the future are also trials of faith. God expects that you will offer Him all of these anxieties so that you can entrust yourself more fully to Him and totally abandon yourself to Him.

Peace Born from Faith

If trials of faith strengthen your self-entrusting to Jesus, your adherence to Him and your reliance on Him, His peace will enter your life. The words 'peace be with you', 'shalom' in Hebrew, is a very intimate greeting which wishes you peace stemming from an intimate communion with God. This is how it was understood in the Old Testament. Christ greets his disciples with this very greeting, 'shalom'. During the Last Supper, He said to them: "Peace I leave with you; my peace I give to you; Not as the world gives do I give to you" (*Jn* 14:27).

The world also wants to give us peace, but only human peace. There are two kinds of peace, just like there are two kinds of happiness. There is human peace and human happiness, both of which are short-lived and temporary. On the other hand there is Christ's peace and Christ's happiness, which are born in us as a permanent reality when based on faith.

What is this human peace and human happiness? It is something we obtain from people. We get it is as though it were given to us out of pity from another person. In other words, looking for this kind of peace and happiness is like begging for scraps. This small bit of human esteem, that hint of praise, a compliment or someone's positive perception of us, are simply scraps which we want to build our peace on. Sometimes a person manages to get what he wanted; he gains others esteem, or becomes successful, and gains this common human scrap which gives him some satisfaction. This is the human peace, begged for, which the world gives. But how fleeting this peace is! It does not take much for our human peace to dissipate and for our happiness to vanish. It is enough that someone is rude to us, is vindictive or gives us a suspicious glance. There is no longer peace within us, because the scraps we begged for are taken from us.

When there is no human peace left, fear, its opposite, appears. Fear promotes sickness, and causes neuroses. Fear is born out of the seeking of human peace. It is a result of losing those bits of peace we begged for and which were taken from us. At other times fear is the consequence of losing someone's esteem, or positive perception of us, or a sincere smile and a small acceptance of our deeds. In this way, we become dependent on human whims and moods, on that which 'makes our day' and on that which the world gives us.

The second peace, *the peace of Christ, flows from His presence*. It is His gift. "My peace I give to you", says Christ. He is our peace given to us through faith (cf. Eph 2:14). *Accepting peace from Christ through faith, is accepting His person; it is totally opening the door of our hearts to Him.*

Anxiety and sadness are always bad and always flowing from self-love. But peace and happiness do not always come from Christ. Not every peace is good, just as not every joy is good. If you are glad that *you yourself* have accomplished something, then this is a human, very short-lived happiness, a piece of scrap. If we strive for this type of happiness and this kind of peace, then it will always be like a bubble, which can be burst without any reason because our Lord does not allow that our human peace, the peace of this world, to be something lasting in our life.

True peace is the fruit of spiritual life, the fruit of faith, deepened as a result of trials. We receive this peace not at the 'start' but at the 'finish'. True peace is not so much the evidence of achievement, but the result of a choice. If there are idols in your life, ties and enslavements that hamper you, there will be no peace. *When something or someone stands between you and God, then you cannot fully adhere to God through faith. Moreover, there will be no peace in you.* It would be a pity for you to succumb to the suffering flowing from this.

The peace of Christ comes as a result of your choosing Him. This basic choice, which is called a fundamental option, is the most important one. Is Christ really of the greatest value to you? He redeemed you on the Cross and was risen, giving you the opportunity to gain true peace and true happiness. This kind of peace involving permanent joy is within your grasp, thanks to the sacrifice on the Cross and the Resurrection. You, however, must make a choice. By taking advantage of the fruits of the Cross and of the Resurrection, you have to choose Christ with His peace. This should be a process of your acceptance of Christ. You cannot, however, choose peace and happiness if you have not chosen Christ. He Himself helps you with this choice, by taking away that which hampers and enslaves you. He overthrows your idols. When you accept this, then this will be your choice, your declaration for peace, happiness and freedom; it will be the choice made by your faith.

If you are a neurotic person and perhaps getting worse, that may mean that there is still not enough of spiritual life in you, your choice of Christ is not complete enough. It may mean that you are still not choosing your Heavenly Friend, and there is still not enough faith which begets peace in you. You have to learn acceptance which is the continuous choosing of Christ. By accepting His will, you choose and accept His love.

In the end, the most important thing, the foundation of this choice is *believing in love*. What does Jesus expect from me, what does He want?

– He wants you, by loving His will, to want what is best for you. Christ does not need anything for Himself. If He does want something from you, then it is always that which is best for you. He wants to love you and wants you to accept His desire which is His love. You are like a small child that does not know what is good for him. A small child needs to be persuaded to study, to eat, to get dressed, as a child does not know how to love itself. It is the mum and dad that love it and care for it. A child is unable to love itself and care for itself. This is the same with us. We do not know what is good for us; we are unable to truly love ourselves. We love ourselves in a pure and unselfish way when we love His will, His love and His concern for us.

Christ is Someone who expects something from you. Primarily He is the Will which reveals Itself to us. *To believe and love Christ is to love what He wants; that is, to love His will.* We are to choose Him in this very way; loving that what He loves. It is only loving the will of Christ, confirmed by our choices during trials of faith, that brings us peace and true happiness which no one can take away from us.

Chapter 4

The Desert

In biblical symbolism, the desert is a stage on the way toward God. All who are called on the path of faith must go through this stage. Abraham went through it when He left Haran, in the Chaldeans, to search for the Promised Land. The history of Moses begins in the desert, when God appears to him in the burning bush and in the quiet of the desert, calls him to the special mission of freeing the Chosen People. Elijah also goes into the desert so as to flee for his life. In order to give Elijah special instructions, God tells him to wander in the desert for 40 days and 40 nights until finally He reveals Himself in a tiny whispering sound in the middle of the desert. God reveals Himself to Elijah not in noise, not in a windstorm or earthquake but in the quiet of nature and in the stillness of his heart. He reveals Himself not in the moment of excitement but in silence, when free from problems and fear, Elijah remains alone with God. God, when speaking through the prophet Hosea, talks about Israel as if it were His chosen bride whom He leads into the desert with love: "So I will allure her; I will lead her into the desert and speak to her heart" (*Hos* 2:16). God, out of His love, leads a person into the desert, as the desert is God's gift. The desert brings about that which St Augustine asked for by saying: Lord, grant that I may know You and that I may know myself.

The Symbolism of the Desert

The desert, as a geographical terrain and as a symbol of a person's situation, does not necessarily in the beginning manifest itself in all its characteristic traits to the full. The geographical desert begins gradually. There is an increasing amount of sand, fewer and fewer trees and more and more dunes. At the beginning, it is possible to find an oasis. This is similar to a human desert. It can be complete, with complete nakedness, with a storm of temptations and a special presence of the merciful God. However, only selected elements of the desert may appear in one's life. Every difficult situation may be a desert in the sense of a trial of faith, which calls one to live by faith. They could be, for example, difficulties arising from a relationship with another person, sickness, a depressing feeling of isolation or another very difficult situation. A desert, *par excellence* (in the fullest sense of its meaning), can be a difficult spiritual state full of dryness for you. Then it may seem as though God has left you, when you do not feel His presence and His presence becomes that much harder to believe in.

The desert can be 'imposed' by God onto a person or onto a community when He Himself leads someone into it, but it can also be a desert out of choice. It may happen that you yourself will desire the situation of a desert to seek out quietness and the presence of God, and you will strive to be stripped of attachments. You will then meet your Enemy there, but you will first and foremost encounter God. *You will be able to look inside your inner self and discover the truth about yourself and, at the same time, discover that which is of the utmost importance – the truth about God.* Jesus, before entering His public life, went first into the desert as if to say to you: "Look, you are not alone, I have been here before you. I was also hungry for forty days and it was hard for me too. You are never alone. Try to believe in my love".

The desert may have a social character. For example, it can be experienced by an entire nation. However, it may also be the desert for an individual person. One thing is certain: *If you enter it, you will change.* It is also certain that *at some point in time you must enter it.* There will be a time when, through internal or external experiences, God will place you in a difficult situation, maybe even an extreme one, in which you will have to choose. You must then remember that this is a grace, the grace of the desert.

If you are presently in a desert such as this, you should be grateful to God. Thank Him that it is difficult for you, that you are sick or lonely or not understood, or maybe life at home or at work is like a nightmare, or that you are unable to cope with yourself. Such situations are the elements of a desert. Try to see that God, who loves you, is present in all of this.

"I Wish You Were either Cold or Hot"

The desert is a place of trial; a place where human attitudes become polarised.

Once four good friends, students, planned to go to the Libyan Desert. They intended to cross it in a Jeep. The events occurred as if in a movie. For the first time they found themselves in a desert, and soon they started to lose their way. Later, a dramatic incident happened, the Jeep broke down and they were at a loss as to what to do next. Their only recourse was to wait to be rescued. The desert, as everybody knows, terrifies and is horrible; especially when there are no future prospects. During the day, it was mercilessly hot, and at night it was intensely cold. In addition, food was getting scarce and there was even less water. Tension, therefore, continued to mount. The remaining water had to be divided among four people. There was so little of it that everybody watched nervously the hands of the one who was pouring it. And then something terrible happened. The hand of the one pouring, most certainly because of the pressure of being watched, trembled and a little water spilled into the sand. The tension and the nervousness of the travelling companions transformed into uncontrolled aggression – How dare you spill it? We will die thanks to you! Then everything came down like an avalanche. Emotions prevailed. The rest of the water was spilled and the bodies of the fighting friends were rolling in the sand. When they finally realised what they were doing, one of them could not get up; he had been suffocated. This indeed, was terrible.

After all that had happened, the arrival of a helicopter which picked up the three living men and the corpse of the fourth, was no longer important to them. What was important was that something terrible had happened between them, that they were no longer the same people. On the Libyan Desert, a murder had been committed among friends, who earlier had thought that they were ready to give up their lives for one another.

The situation of a desert reveals that which is deeply hidden in a person. It reveals the layers of human passions and evil that manifest themselves only in difficult situations. Hence the desert uncovers a person and reveals the truth about him. In the desert, a person sees what his powerlessness, sinfulness, and unrepentant heart is capable of. *A person here stands face to face with the terrifying truth of who he really is without the visible power of God.* The barrenness of the desert uncovers the wretchedness of a person and reveals his nakedness because his illusions dissipate, and there is nowhere to hide. A person can live skin deep, as if on the surface of his own self. It is not until the arrival of difficult situations and the experience of the desert which forces him to make decisions, that the deep layers of good or evil are revealed.

The desert not only reveals the truth about yourself but it also transforms you internally, and polarises your attitudes. *The gift of the desert lets you overcome lukewarmness*, because the desert forces you to make choices. By making choices, you will become aware of what you are capable of and thereby you will come to understand the two most important realities: the reality of the incomprehensible love and infinite mercy of God, as well as the reality of your own sinfulness and helplessness. *As long as you are a lukewarm Christian* for whom everything goes well and for whom there are no problems, *your situation as seen in the light of faith is tragic*. It is so bad because you manage your life yourself, and you no longer need God. This is a situation of practical atheism which you may not even be aware of.

The ultimate reason for leading a human being, a nation or a community into the desert is revealed by the very clearly expressed words of the Revelation: "I know your works; I know that you are neither cold nor hot. I wish you were either cold or hot. So, because you are lukewarm, I will spit you out of my mouth" (*Rev* 3:15-16).

God finds lukewarmness in a person unacceptable. It is something repulsive that He cannot tolerate within you and for that reason, sooner or later, He has to lead you to the desert. The circumstances in the desert polarise ones attitudes and cause one to become either hot or cold and no longer lukewarm.

Moses, the great saint of the Old Testament, and others were sanctified in the desert whereas some became murderers, criminals, and idolaters. The Fathers of the Church claim that God leads a person to the desert in order for him to believe, or to blaspheme; *either faith or blasphemy, but not indifference.* That is how it was in the biblical desert. Many blasphemed against God, and others were sanctified. The gift of the desert does not allow one to maintain the masked attitude of atheism.

The experience of the desert will allow you to understand how senseless is the judgement of one person toward another. This will help you to fight against all of your judgements toward others. What do you know anyway about another person that you meet along your road and in whom you may see a great deal of evil? It is his existential situation that is of prime importance. He could be experiencing trials or he could be in the desert stage. Thus, you must not allow any judgement of another person to be formed.

The desert is a privileged place for Satan, since a person is then weak and easily succumbs to temptation. Satan takes advantage of this situation. The desert can also, in this way, increase the chance of rebellion. There were particularly strong temptations and revolts in the desert which the Chosen People crossed. Dramatic situations arose resulting in leading men turning away from God, even to the point of starting the cult of the golden calf.

A person is transformed in the desert, he becomes different since a true polarisation of attitudes is brought about. He therefore becomes either better or worse. A person can become a criminal, but he can also become a saint.

The Desert as a Place of Denudation

The Biblical symbolism of the desert is closely connected to God's call for the Chosen People to leave Egypt and to enter the Promised Land. The road from Egypt to Canaan is about four hundred kilometres long. Even a caravan numbering in the thousands could cross that desert in two or three weeks. And yet, the journey of the Chosen People lasted fourty years. God, by calling His people into the desert forced them to rid themselves of self-assurance and to submit to a hard life. God called them to submit to the *process of denudation, being stripped of supports and attachments,* which is necessary on the road to faith and to total abandonment to God.

The desert is primarily *a symbol of denudation*. Man stands before the limitless sky, the limitless sand and before himself. Everything is reduced to the primary and essential elements – open space, the sky, the earth, sand, God and man himself. Entering the desert means being stripped of basic things and hunger and thirst torment both physically and spiritually. Denudation gives rise to physical and spiritual hunger and thirst, both of which are inseparable from each other. In these difficulties that which has been deeply hidden within a person is brought to the surface.

The desert is the place and time for separating oneself from attachments, from one's own systems of security. A person wandering in the desert has nothing. His life's situation is uncertain, he has no securities, he lacks everything. He who crosses the desert experiences the necessity of being satisfied with what he receives from God and the necessity for awaiting everything from Him. He experiences the necessity of relying solely on God, because *God wants to become everything for the traveller through the desert*.

The wandering nation which received the miraculous manna from God, could not collect more than it needed for a day. The people had to believe anew each day that the manna would fall. They had to believe that God would incessantly take care of them. *The desert, therefore, is a place where faith is born. Faith deepens to the extent of denudation.* God will fill a person with His presence to the extent that this person will denude himself and will desire to answer God's call, thus opening himself to the love he experiences.

The more a person allows himself to be stripped of his own 'self' and of his own securities, the more God can descend into him and be the only One for him to rely on. *God reminds us that the more this mutual, mysterious relationship between Him and ourselves deepens, the greater becomes the need for our denudation* which is a way of God's calling us fervently to make a more complete gift of ourselves to Him. God expects that the one who loves Him will want to go beyond his human capabilities. He will agree to be totally stripped of all that he is and of all that he possesses, in order that he may become a sign, so that God can become a living presence in the world through him.

The desert is a birthplace of faith which becomes ever more dynamic. This kind of faith transforms a person's life. In the desert, God expects a lukewarm person of little faith, to become zealous in faith and in self-surrender to the Lord. It was because of the denudation of the people in the desert, that the Covenant was made there and that the vows between Israel and God were made. Then God became a gift for the people and the people promised their gift of faithfulness to God.

The Desert as an Experience of God's Love

The denudation which a person experiences in the desert, together with knowing the truth about himself, allows him to come to know the truth about God, who is love. The desert enables him to experience God's presence and power in a special way. Above all it allows him to experience His mercy. *God responds to sin and to human weakness with love and fatherly concern*. To people that rebel and sin He responds with the miracles of manna and water so desperately needed by them. Despite the human evil, which manifests itself more clearly in the desert, God is present there in a special way. He led the Chosen People. God was visible, while at the same time hidden in a column of cloud and in a column of fire. The column of cloud, which indicated the presence of God, at the same time, hid Him. For the Israelites, the column of cloud was both light and darkness; it symbolised that God was close to them and yet unreachable.

God led an unorganised crowd into the desert. However, those who crossed it were already a nation united with God through the Covenant, they were a transformed people. The purpose of a desert is the formation of a person by strengthening his faith, eliminating mediocrity and forming a true disciple of Christ. The Chosen People entered the Promised Land as a small community, but one rich in the experience of the desert. They experienced God amid threatening situations like violent storms with thunder and lightening, while at the same time, they experienced their own weakness and their own failure. They experienced with unusual clarity their own wretchedness and that is why they experienced God's mercy so greatly.

In the desert, you come to know God who never abandons you. It is true that God hides Himself in the desert, but in reality He is very close to you. God is never closer to you than He is then. He waits only for your faith. He waits for you in faith, to stretch out your arms to Him.

The Chosen People discovered in their own weakness the true mystery of God. *If you experience your weakness, then you are called by God to throw yourself into His merciful arms*. You experience the desert in your life so that you will turn towards the One who is mercy Himself.

Experiencing the desert will help you to discover the need for God and to know that you are completely dependent on Him. During this time, when you will go through very difficult hours of discouragement, temptation and darkness, you will better understand your own helplessness and powerlessness. When you discover the truth about yourself and ask God for forgiveness, you will find, just as the Prodigal Son did, great tenderness in the Father and His extreme joy upon your return. You will be able to look into His eyes full of love. In forgiving you, God will, at the same time, bring about humility within you.

The desert is not a dwelling place; it is only *a path, a road on which one comes to know the merciful love of God*. Everyone who seeks God must pass along it, since the experience of the desert is closely related to the deepening of our faith in His mercy.

A desert experience is a time when a person becomes formed, according to the rule that only that, which is difficult and gives resistance, moulds a person. The love of God, which is then born in you, should finally become communion with God. St John of the Cross states: "[...] for to love is to labour to divest and deprive oneself for God of all that is not God" (*The Ascent of Mount Carmel* II, 5, 7). *The desert* is not only a place where our faith is born, but it ultimately *becomes the birthplace and dwelling place of our contemplation.*

Going through the desert in your life *you will always meet Mary.* She will be close to you, and will look at you with motherly tenderness and concern. The one who is the Mediatrix of Graces and the Mediatrix of Mercy, will intercede for you to God. She will look at you anxiously, to see whether you follow her example and say your 'fiat', your 'yes', and whether you see God in the situations which you experience. The Chosen People did not have Mary with them. She is with you, that is why you will never walk alone. The one who experienced so many difficult situations will walk before you. She will be your light and will show you the road to her Son. Her presence will shine in the darkness of your desert.

Chapter 5

Rich and Humble Temporal Means within the Church

Jacques Maritain divides temporal means which may be used for spiritual ends, into two categories: *rich temporal means* and *humble temporal means* (cf. J. Maritain, *On the Philosophy of History*, 1957, p. 70). Those means which are visible and can be statistically analysed Maritain calls 'rich' means. They are tangible things like organisations, meetings, marches, church architecture and decoration, audio-visual aids and mass media means. A characteristic trait of 'rich means' is their influence on one's self-love because their effects and results are apparent. This has the danger of our claiming these results as our own, and as a result, of our adopting an attitude of triumph.

According to Maritain, the second type of means are 'humble' means. They are marked with the stigma of the Cross and express one of the most profound truths in the Gospel: "[...] unless a grain of wheat falls to the ground and dies, it remains a grain of wheat; but if it dies, it produces much fruit" (*Jn* 12:24). In these means, a true paradox of the dynamism of faith can be observed: the poorer they are, that is the more destitute, the more insignificant in themselves and the less visible, the more efficacious they are. As opposed to 'rich means', these 'humble means' are not dependant on tangible success, and they do not have any internal need for temporal success.

The Poverty of Jesus

In our lives and in the Church we are used to relying on 'rich means'. We so very much desire to see the victory and triumph of Christ and to see His might and authority. Meanwhile, He is hidden; He is poor in Bethlehem, even poorer on Mount Calvary and maybe He is poorest of all in the Eucharist. By going to such an extreme in His poverty and humility, He emphasises the importance of 'humble means'.

Jesus, in His redeeming works, above all, chooses poor and 'humble means'. No evidence of power is present at His birth. He comes to us as a small Child, completely dependent on the people around Him. He resists no one. Neither can He do what He wants nor can He defend Himself. Above all, He lets Himself be known through his lowliness, humility and weakness. *This is how He appeared at the moment of His birth and this is how He was in His Passion.* He showed that you too must be stripped of everything. He showed that you must die to yourself like a grain of wheat, choosing that which is most effective: the 'humble means'.

This does not mean that Jesus did not use 'rich means'. The triumphant arrival into Jerusalem is certainly a rich means; it is the triumph of Christ. Jesus wanted to show that if He so wishes, crowds will give Him great homage and will lay their cloaks before Him. By this, He wanted to show that He could do anything. But this event could have misled the Apostles. In order for the Apostles to remain sober in their thoughts, on Palm Sunday, right after His triumphant arrival into Jerusalem, Jesus said the following shocking words: "Amen, amen I say to you, unless a grain of wheat falls to the ground and dies, it remains a grain of wheat; but if it dies, it produces much fruit" (*Jn* 12:24).

There were miracles in the life of Jesus such as the transfiguration on Mount Tabor, but above all He used 'humble means'. During His arrest, once again we see 'rich means' used by Him, the guards had to fall on their faces before Him upon hearing His words (cf. *Jn* 18:6). He threw them to the ground and showed them His power and might. Later, however, He allowed them to ridicule and scorn Him. He allowed them to spit on Him and to shout at Him on the Cross: "Aha! You, who would destroy the temple and re-

build it in three days, save yourself by coming down from
the cross. ...He saved others, but he cannot save himself"
(*Mk* 15:29-31). Jesus, with all His Divine calmness accepts
all of this and takes up these 'humble means' to save the
world.

The Efficacy of 'Humble Means'

'Humble means' is the acceptance of suffering out of love
for God. You encounter such means when your knees hurt
during prayer, when you deny yourself something, when
you question who you are and at times live in great calmness, silence, and contemplation. Nothing much is known
about these things; they are invisible means. They cannot
be measured by any sociological statistics. However, these
are the 'humble means' that in the light of faith, prove to be
the deciding factor in the fate of the world.

'Rich means' are the ones that are rich in the eyes of the
world but they are seen differently in the light of faith. "For
the foolishness of God is wiser than human wisdom",
St Paul says, "and the weakness of God is stronger than
human strength" (*1 Cor* 1:25). That which is humble in the
eyes of people, is rich in the eyes of God. *The richest, therefore, are 'humble means'. They are the most effective.
They are an indication of true wisdom, the wisdom of
the Gospel*. The use of 'rich means' will only be effective
when rooted in 'humble means' – in a deep spiritual life, in
a life of prayer, in dying to oneself, and in total devotion to
God. The efficacy of 'humble means' stems from the presence of Christ in the soul, according to the rule, that God is
devoted to the soul as much as it is devoted to Him. The
works of an active life, as St Thomas Aquinas says, are born
of the fullness of contemplation (*Summa theologica*, 2, 2,
qu. 188). The efficacy of 'rich means' (the juristic-organisa-
tional apostolate) flows from the richness of 'humble means',
and not otherwise. 'Rich means' can be limited by external
factors, for example by the lack of time, physical strength,

organisational management, or by persecution of the Church. 'Humble means' cannot be taken from the Church by outside factors. Their lack cannot be justified, since to use them one needs only good will and love.

'Rich means' are also necessary to the Church and they should not be rejected. God does not want one-sidedness of the apostleship. For example, He wants a Catholic press and a variety of visible forms of this apostolate to exist. St Maximillian Kolbe is in a certain sense a patron of 'rich means'. He dreamed about seeing a million magazines of "Rycerz Niepokalanej" ("Knight of the Immaculate") go out into the world – and his dream came true. It was Father Kolbe who gave out miraculous medals of the Immaculate in the streets of Japanese cities. He dreamed about a radio station, about planes and ships in the service of the Immaculate. These 'rich means' should not be disregarded and should also be involved in service to the Lord. We have to remember, however, that *their efficacy flows from the presence of 'humble means'.*

St Maximillian was a man of success, so many things turned out well for him. He founded a large apostolic Marian centre named *Niepokalanów* (this means: Town of the Immaculate) near Warsaw in Poland, which became a source of amazement for the entire Church. He founded similar centres of the Immaculate on other continents, also named *Niepokalanów*. This undoubted success was gained only through 'humble means'. St Maximillian gives the following testimony about this: "When all other means failed, when they all thought that there was no hope left for me, and my superiors concluded that I was good for nothing, then the Immaculate picked up this instrument, which was only good enough for the rubbish heap" (M. Winowska, *Szaleniec Niepokalanej*, p.71). It was Mary, to whom Father Maximillian was totally devoted, who picked up this little 'nothing' in order to make use of him to spread the glory of God and to save souls. The efficacy of his apostleship and his work in the service of the Immaculate began when he became gravely ill. His brothers and superiors then claimed, that because he was in an advanced stage of tuberculosis he was no longer fit to work and then they all had their doubts about him. Then he was stripped of everything, like the grain of wheat which must die in order to bear fruit. This is a Divine paradox. A man, who was considered useless in human terms, became a most effective instrument in God's hands, because *it was God who lived in him and acted through him. It was God who achieved success through this saint.*

Faith is the acknowledgement of one's own helplessness and the awaiting of everything from God. **This experience of helplessness and awaiting of everything from God are** *par excellence* '**humble means**'. Do you see the value of humble means in your life? God certainly does not limit your opportunities of this kind. Who among us does not undergo moments of torment, some particular difficulties or moments of spiritual deserts? Who among us does not have problems with our own selves and with external conditions of life? All of this cannot be seen, classified, or evaluated. It is so unnoticeable, that one cannot find any statistical data on this subject. Who could possibly know that at a certain point in your life you said 'yes' to God: "I do want – I want everything that You expect from me". Who could know, that at a certain point when it was very hard for you, you said through tears that you love Him and always want to love Him? Who knows how many times you vanquished your own self, denied yourself something, and overcame your own will? *It is these 'humble means' that are of the utmost importance to you, to the Church and to the world; these are the means that summon the might of God.* How many times has God given you the opportunity to take advantage of them? Maybe you wasted these opportunities or refused to accept these priceless gifts from God. Maybe you even resented them and rebelled, while He almost forced them on you and asked you not to refuse that which is so important to the salvation of the world. St Maximillian Kolbe, who was called God's Beggar, best knew the value of 'humble means'. You must not forget that it is very important for you to accept humiliation with joy.

Try to smile in spite of feeling sad, and, in spite of your experiences, you try to look at the world cheerfully and with the faith that love will certainly conquer all. God appreciates everything. The efforts you make when you kneel on hard floor and your knees hurt very much, when you stand in a crowded church and your legs are painful, or when you are tired with a long drive to church in bad weather. He knows all about the humble means He has given to you for your use, which in the depth of your heart, you decide to accept or reject. It is in your heart, that your own fate is determined and the fate of those closest to you. *Since 'humble means' by themselves do not guarantee your reaching your life's goal, the efficacy of 'humble means' is based on faith, therefore, this efficacy is the evidence that it is God Himself who is acting.*

You may say that you pray a great deal for someone who does not believe, for someone's conversion or for someone's health. But everything depends on how you pray. Sometimes, your one 'yes' spoken to God with joy would suffice. This simple, unassuming means can really perform miracles. If you find it hard to accept God's invitation to participate in the saving of souls, think about John Paul II, about his crown of thorns in the form of being viciously criticised and his great fatigue especially when travelling so often around the world. Think about St Maximillian, for whom so many things worked out, only as the result of 'humble means'.

He so very often found it difficult to breathe; especially during his travels where he was actually suffocating. He writes in his letters that sometimes he simply couldn't breathe and was totally exhausted. His devotion to the Immaculate was called a folly, but it was his determination in using 'humble means' that was the true folly.

If you have not understood the value of 'humble means', then you do not understand the depth of Christianity at all. If you do not understand the value and sense of 'humble means', then you do not understand the Cross which, of course, is at the centre of the Church.

It was from the Cross that Jesus drew everything to Himself. It was under this Cross that His mother stood and did not take back her "yes" when faced with the terrible suffering of the Saviour. It is from the Cross that God's grace of redemption and sanctification of the world flows continuously.

The Saviour draws you to Himself not by His triumphant entrance to Jerusalem but by the Cross. It is from the Cross that He calls you to follow Him and to love Him as He has loved you,"to the end".

The patroness of 'humble means' is Mary, who, if judged from the human perspective, did not accomplish any great deed in her lifetime. There are no rich means in her life at all; there is poverty, silence, a hidden life, humility, obedience, prayer, contemplation and devotion to God. Her life, filled with simplicity and the use of 'humble means', was a life *hidden within God*. She invites you also, to this kind of life. She wants you to live a life of faith, so that in your heart you will desire to use 'humble means', thus imitating her life in Nazareth. She wants you to see the truth of this statement of St John of the Cross: "For a little of this pure love is more precious to God and the soul and more beneficial to the Church, [...] than all these other works put together" (*The Spiritual Canticle*, Stanza XXIX, 2; *The Collected Works of St John of the Cross*, Washington, D.C. 1991, p.587).

Victory through Faith

The battle with the Amelekites is the classic Biblical scene which shows the value and sense of 'humble means' in the light of faith. While crossing the desert on the road to the Promised Land, the Israelites engaged in battle with the Amelekites, because the Amelekites controlled the routes through the desert (cf. Ex 17:8-13). Moses, a man of God, knew how to guarantee a victory for his troops. If he were a strategist who thought only in human terms, according to the rules of military strategy, he himself, would have stood at the head of his troops. If he had taken leadership himself, he surely would have encouraged his troops, since they were so devoted to him. However, he did something which was absurd from a point of view of military strategy. He retreated and left his army under the control of Joshua, his second in command. Then he climbed to the top of the hill to pray there. Moses, as a man of God and a man of prayer, knew very well who decides the fate of the world and the fate of his nation. This is why Moses stood on the top of the hill with his arms outstretched in a gesture of faith. There was a close connection between him and the valley where the battle was raging. When his arms tired, his army retreated. He knew what this meant – *God wanted him always to put forth an effort, to incessantly stretch out his arms to the Lord*. Aaron and Hur, who accompanied Moses, supported his arms when they became completely numb. So it was throughout the entire day that this gesture of outstretched arms to God, accompanied the Israelites' battle. Finally, when night came, victory was theirs. However, it was not Joshua or his army, which fought in the valley who were victorious. In fact, it was Moses praying on the hill, who was victorious. It was his faith that was victorious.

If this scene were to take place in our times, then the attention of the journalists, the television cameras, and the spotlights would be directed towards the place where Joshua was fighting. It would seem to us that this is that place where everything would be decided. Who among us would have paid attention to a single, praying man? *But it was this single man who was victorious because God was victorious through his faith.*

Moses' outstretched arms are a symbol that says it is God who decides everything. He, who rules, is there; everything depends on Him. Human capabilities can be ridiculously small, but for the Lord, nothing is impossible to achieve. *The gesture of outstretched arms*, those numbed arms, *is a gesture of faith. It is a 'humble means' which expresses the folly of faith in the infinite might and boundless love of the Lord.*

Spiritual Motherhood

Spiritual motherhood is brought about through humble means since it is realised by participating in the death of Christ: "unless a grain of wheat falls to the ground and dies, it remains a grain of wheat". Following that, it is brought about through participating in His Resurrection: "but if it dies, it produces much fruit". Sharing in the death of Christ is brought about primarily by accepting suffering because it kills egoism. On the other hand, sharing in the Resurrection, is putting on a "new self created in God's way" (Eph 4:24) in the likeness of Christ, who is Love. It is the apostleship of begetting Christ in souls. It means that the apostle shares Christ who is present in his soul. According to St Paul, the apostleship is a spiritual fatherhood which, in the essence, is the same as spiritual motherhood: "[...] for I became your father in Christ Jesus through the Gospel" (*1 Cor* 4:15). Our apostleship as spiritual motherhood, is, due to faith, our partaking in the spiritual motherhood of the Church. *Through our faith, which fully manifests itself by the use of humble means, souls are reborn to live for Christ*. Spiritual motherhood is brought about through the living word, which is the fruit of contemplative contact with God. It is brought about through prayerful devotion to God, and particularly through sacrifice and suffering.

Two great sinners played a special role in the life of St Thérèse of the Child Jesus. When she was fourteen she learned about one of them, Pranzini who had murdered three people. Despite being sentenced to death, he showed no remorse. Thérèse could not come to terms with the thought that he might die without being reconciled with God. For a month and a half, she offered all of her prayers and suffering for Pranzini. Then God gave her a sign: this great sinner, in the last moment before his death, took a Crucifix and kissed the wounds of the Saviour three times. When Thérèse learned about this, full of emotion, she said to Celine, *"This is my first son."* Thérèse, being only fourteen already had such a clear understanding of spiritual motherhood. She writes later, "[...] suffering alone can give birth to souls for Jesus [...]" (*Letter to Celine*, July 8, 1891). Pranzini was a prototype of all sinners, whom Thérèse wanted to pray for in a special way and for whom she wanted to offer her suffering. She knew that prayer alone was not enough, that, in order to save souls one has to offer the greatest gift for God, one's own suffering.

A more dramatic figure of a great sinner, according to testimonies of St Thérèse, was Fr. Hyacinthe Loyson. His name is never mentioned either in her autobiography, in Thérèse's letters, or in the *Story of a Soul*. Only twice, in her letters to Celine, does she mention "a certain Lily faded and withered" and that "he is really culpable" (*Letter to Celine*, April 26, 1891; July 8th, 1891). We find out about her desire to save this soul from the records of the process of beatification and canonisation. Hyacinthe Loyson, a Discalced Carmelite, superior of the convent in Paris, was a great and unusually gifted preacher whose conferences moved audiences in all of France. Even the Pope congratulated him on his successes. But, at certain point in time this exceptionally religious man turned from being a great preacher into becoming an apostate – a fighting apostate. He started to travel across the dioceses in France and, despite many protestations, he preached that the Church had moved away from the true Gospel. He fought the Church in this way for forty-three years. This battle terrified the convent in Lisieux, so much so that no one had the courage to mention his name. He was never directly mentioned, and that is why his name never appears in the writings of St Thérèse, who was offering her prayers and sufferings for his intention during nine years. For Pranzini, a month and a half was enough for his conversion, whereas for Fr. Loyson, nine years seemed to be insufficient. Father Loyson was excommunicated and later wrote an open letter incriminating the Church and the Carmelite Order. This provoked vehement protests and great indignation. Thérèse, however, did not lose hope. With a beating heart she said to Celine that his conversion was her main desire. "Dear Celine, he is really culpable, more culpable than any other sinner who was ever converted. But cannot Jesus do once what He has not yet ever done? And if He were not to desire it, would He have placed in the heart of His poor little spouses a desire that He could not realise?" (*Letter to Celine*, July 8th, 1891). This is her often-repeated statement, that if Jesus gives us the desire for something then it is not meant to remain unfulfilled. "No, it is certain", she writes, "that He desires more than we do to bring back this poor stray sheep to the fold. A day will come when He will open his eyes [...]" (ibid.).

When we analyse St Thérèse's faith, we see that her faith was a certainty. She knew that Hyacinthe Loyson would be converted: "Let us not grow tired of prayer"; she wrote, "confidence works miracles. [...] It is not our merits but those of our Spouse, which are ours, that we offer to our Father who is in heaven, in order that our brother, a son of the Blessed Virgin, may return vanquished to throw himself beneath the mantle of the most merciful of Mothers [...]" (ibid.). Thérèse so desired to save his soul that she offered her last Holy Communion for his intention. She died fully realising that Fr. Hyacinthe Loyson was not converted, but the certainty of her faith remained unshaken. The priest did die fifteen years later aged eighty-five. Jesus loved Thérèse so much, that this time He did not have to give her any sign. Jesus knew that she would not stop believing that Fr. Loyson would be converted. When in 1912 Loyson was dying, there was no Catholic priest with him and there was no confession. It is known, however, that before his death he received a copy of a *Story of a Soul* and read the writings of St Thérèse in one reading, which he described as "a folly and something quite shocking". During his difficult death, those close to him heard the words "Oh, my sweet Jesus" repeated (cf. *Letters of St Thérèse of Lisieux*, vol. II, p.731). This last act of love directed towards Jesus allows us to assume that Fr. Hyacinthe was saved – thanks to the prayers and sufferings of Thérèse. He was also her spiritual son.

This statement by St Thérèse "[...] suffering alone can give birth to souls for Jesus [...]" shows us what spiritual motherhood depends on. A mother is one who gives life and who supports that life. A person fears suffering, but none of us can free ourselves from it, just as we cannot free ourselves from the burden of each day. However the advantage of our suffering and difficulties can be wasted. Only by accepting them and linking them with the Cross of Jesus will allow us to enter the extraordinary mystery of spiritual motherhood. *Taking part in the royal priesthood of the faithful, we are called to this kind of motherhood. We are to gain and give birth to souls for Jesus.* Think about all the many things that are difficult for you: maybe the lack of health, domestic conflicts, rebellious children or some spiritual torment. These things could be of even less significance, but if they are accepted and offered, they cause you to participate in the spiritual motherhood of the Church which means giving birth to souls for Christ. *There is nothing more important than this.* This motherhood can be brought about by a verbal apostolate and by an apostolate of prayer. However, suffering is the most effective means. Moreover, it is the most effective form of apostleship, since the greatest nakedness, which is a 'humble means', is found in suffering. In it there is a minimum of you and the maximum of Christ – *in suffering, the Cross is most truly outstretched.*

The Testimony of John Paul II

On May 25th 1985, in St Peter's Square in Rome, Pope John Paul II placed a cardinal's biretta on the head of Archbishop Andrzej Maria Deskur. This was an unusual consistory which invoked shock and amazement. Why was the Pope appointing a paralysed man as Cardinal? Surely, the Cardinal dignity is not a title or award for the work of a bishop. Cardinals are the first advisers and associates of the Pope. They have a very important role in the Church. Why then was a man, unable to work because of his suffering, appointed Cardinal? John Paul II discreetly revealed this mystery in the evening of the consistory in his speech to pilgrims from Poland. This is what he said about Cardinal Deskur: "He is particularly close to me from long ago, in my student years in the seminary, throughout the years of my priesthood and through many meetings in Rome, but especially throughout the last meeting before the conclave. Then the Providence of God touched Bishop Deskur with this extreme handicap, which he has until today. Among all the cardinals appointed today, he is the only one in a wheelchair and brings into this College of Cardinals a special stigma, the stigma of suffering which is a sacrifice. We do not know the ways of God; we do not know God's mysteries, but it is hard for me, personally, not to be convinced that the sacrifice of Archbishop, now Cardinal Andrzej, happened in connection with the conclave which took place in the middle of October, 1978". In the suffering of Archbishop Andrzej Deskur, the Holy Father saw the price that was paid so that he, Cardinal Wojtyła could become the successor of Christ. We know that as soon as the Pope was elected, his first steps were directed toward the Gemelli clinic where the sick and paralysed Archbishop Andrzej Maria Deskur laid. He was the one to whom the Pope, according to his own opinion, owed so much. The Pope had gone to meet the one, who had given the Pope the 'better part' – his help through suffering, a difficult part, but the most effective like all humble means. The fact that the disabled Archbishop Andrzej Maria Deskur was appointed Cardinal is an indirect indication by John Paul II of the value of humble means.

Cardinal Deskur was previously the head of the Papal Commission for Mass Media. Thus, he was in charge of the distribution and of the function of 'rich means' within the Church. He did much in this field. He contributed a great deal toward preparing documents of the Church, which laid out the way of action for the Catholic Mass Media. However, the Pope did not mention these merits. He said nothing about the greatness of Cardinal Deskur's contribution for the development of the Mass Media. The Cardinal brought with him into the College of Cardinals the stigma of suffering, which is a sacrifice. One gets the impression that, in this way, the Pope wanted to emphasise the value of humble means.

On the first of June in the afternoon, Cardinal Andrzej Maria Deskur received his titular Church of San Cesareo in Palatio; the same church that was received by Cardinal Karol Wojtyła in 1967. The Cardinal, in the majesty of his suffering, celebrated Mass seated. Instead of a cardinal's throne, there stood an armchair on wheels by a low altar. His hand, crippled by the illness, held the crosier with difficulty. A peculiar paradox; the head of the Papal Commission in matters of rich means was marked by the stigma of humble means.

The words of John Paul II regarding the attempt on his life should also be understood in the context of the doctrine of 'humble means'. He called that incident a particular grace. On October 14th 1981, during the Wednesday general audience in St Peter's Square, while speaking to thousands of pilgrims, he said these significant words: "God allowed me to experience suffering through the past months, allowed me to experience my life in peril, and allowed me at the same time to understand clearly and profoundly that this is His special grace for myself as a person. It is a grace for the Church as well, since I serve as successor of St Peter. Christ gave me this grace that I may give testimony of His love through suffering and through the danger to my life and health. I find this to be a particular grace and for this I offer special thanksgiving to the Holy Spirit and to the Immaculate Virgin Mary".

Without 'humble means', without the suffering which marked his life, could John Paul II have so effectively been the shepherd of the Church? Could he have drawn crowds? The Pope mentions the dramatic days of the attempt on his life once more on his Saint's feastday, November 4th 1981: "The incident on the 13th of May gave me a great deal to think about and made me look even more, in the light of the Gospel, at my human and Christian life according to those words about the grain that must die so that it can bear fruit".

Part Three
The Actualisation of Faith

*Faith should permeate our whole life. Then, through it, the one who has faith, enters into a relationship with God with all his humanity and all his everyday life. Faith is most fully actualised through the sacraments, especially through the sacraments of Christian initiation. It is because of faith that we can see the redeeming works of Christ in those sacraments and accept them. **Baptism** is the first sacrament of Christian initiation. In this sacrament we receive the gift of faith together with the gift of supernatural life. In a baptised person, a fundamental consecration is brought about through the incorporation into Christ. This consecration means that a person is offered to God and is called to holiness. **Confirmation**, as the second sacrament of Christian initiation, intensifies the dynamism of faith, enriches the baptised with a special strength of the Holy Spirit and emphasises his responsibility for spreading and defending the faith. Moreover, through the **Eucharist**, which is the sacrament of the culmination of our faith and the third sacrament of initiation. we can be intimately united with the crucified and Risen Christ. Partaking in the redemptive sacrifice of Christ is the sum-*

mit of life in faith. United with the sacrifice of Christ, we offer ourselves to God the Father. The Eucharist, during which together we make our offering and are united with Christ, creates a community of faith.

*Faith is being actualised through prayer in a particular way, since **prayer**, which is initiated and developed through faith, is the dialogue between man and God the Father through Jesus Christ in the Holy Spirit. Faith is also brought about by **listening intently to the Word of God**, which is the form of dialogue with Him. In this dialogue a person willingly entrusts himself to God. A person shows compliance of intellect and will, by obedience in faith to God, who then reveals Himself. It is also necessary for faith to be expressed in deeds of **love**, without which it is dead. Faith, as a permanent process of being converted, is an incessant opening of oneself to the love of God and is the continual acceptance of this love so that it can be bestowed on others.*

Chapter 1

The Sacrament of Baptism

Baptism is the summit of the actualisation of faith, as are the other sacraments. Baptism is the foundation and the beginning of this process; it is a beginning of fullness of life in Christ (UR 22). In conciliar thought, the Sacrament of Baptism as all the other sacraments was named the sacrament of faith. All the sacraments require faith, presume that faith is present and are a sign of faith, while at the same time allow faith to grow. Faith precedes Baptism and leads to it. Faith is the disposition of the soul to receive Baptism.

Through Baptism, death to sin is brought about in us. This is a real death, a destruction in a person of that which was evil and unredeemed in him, *so that he may be reborn as a son of God, becoming a new creature, a "partaker in the divine nature" (LG 40), who is called to holiness*. Through Baptism a person is offered and consecrated to God; he becomes His true worshiper and His adopted child. Vatican II, when speaking about Baptism, reveals truths to us that are beyond human intellect and imagination. It speaks of our incorporation into the crucified and glorified Christ, and of conforming ourselves to His image. It says that through Baptism, man receives a gift of faith and from then on, partakes in the royal priesthood of Christ. Through this, he becomes a partaker in His priestly, prophetic and royal ministry, and is incorporated, although not yet completely – in His Mystical Body.

The Immersion into the Death and Resurrection of Christ

Because of little faith, Baptism remains the sacrament not yet fully appreciated by Christians. Deep faith is needed to understand the words of St Paul: "For you have died, and your life is hidden with Christ in God" (*Col* 3:3). Paul's expression "have died" has the same meaning as the words used by the Apostle in his Letter to the Romans when he writes about the importance of the sacrament of Baptism leading us into the Life of Christ: "Or are you unaware that we who are baptised in Christ were baptised into his death?" (*Rom* 6:3). It is due to the consequence of His death, that we enter a new life through baptism. This first sacrament of the Church is the beginning of our being "hidden with Christ in God". *Baptism is the origin and source of faith.* It begins in us a supernatural life which is a life of faith, hope and love.

From then on we are buried with Christ for sin, for moral evil and for everything that is not Christ-like. This is a true death, because all attachments to the world and to any other value besides God, must die within us, so that we may enter a new life, which begun in the Resurrection of Christ.

In every religious system, the phenomenon of double birth occurs. A person is born not only in the physical sense, but also in the spiritual sense. Birth in a spiritual sense is a kind of initiation. In certain non-Christian religions, these initiations have been developed into extremely dramatic forms, based on the symbolism of death and re-birth. These forms are dramatic because their symbolism takes advantage of that which terrifies one in death and of that which is considered wonderful in a new life. Many of these dramatised forms revert to strong symbolism and images such as being buried in the ground, being thrown through an opening surrounded by burning torches, being devoured by a mythical monster or actually being buried with a dead body. This is all done to shake one up and to cause one an emotional shock, which deeply affects the human imagination. In the non-Christian systems, the initiation is based only on the imagination, as only the imagination can be attracted by it.

In Christianity, initiation,understood as a birth into a supernatural life, is brought about by three sacraments: Baptism, Confirmation and the Eucharist. The symbolism and sacramental signs in these sacraments relate to faith and not to the imagination. It would be inadequate to relate the sacraments to the imagination, since the denotation of sacramental signs is beyond all human thought and imagination.

Through Baptism, it is as if a new, supernatural organism is grafted into the human nature. A new life is grafted into one's life. If a scientist was able to successfully transplant animal life into something that previously had only a vegetative life (for example, a plant), the world would be greatly amazed. Observing an experiment such as this, people would be shocked when perceiving that a plant begins to see, hear, feel, and react to sound. It would most certainly be declared the greatest miracle of human genius. Meanwhile, this transplantation brought about in the sacrament of Baptism is beyond all imagination much more significant than the above mentioned fictional transplantation of a new type of life.

When we look at the sacramental signs of water being poured on an infant's or adult catechumen's head, at the anointing of the head with the sacred chrism, and the giving of the candle and white garment; these signs are not able to reveal to us the reality of what is being brought about. A person is not capable of fathoming it without faith. *Only living faith allows us to see the redeeming action of Christ in Baptism and to accept it.*

Baptism allows us to share in the absolutely new life which Christ began in the history of mankind through His Resurrection. This newness of life is our freedom from the legacy of sin, from its 'enslavement', and is our sanctification in truth. *It is the discovering of God's call to be united with Him and to live with Christ in Him.* This newness has within itself the beginnings of all human vocations. Ultimately, every call, be it a call to the priesthood, or to religious life or to fatherhood or motherhood, leads towards the full actualisation of the sacrament of Baptism.

Dying with Christ, which is initiated at Baptism, allows us to partake in the fruits of His resurrection, like the seed which must die in order to bear fruit which is new life. *Through Baptism, a fundamental consecration is brought about, the offering of a human being to God to belong only to Him.* This consecration can be brought about thanks to the graces of Christ's Redemption, and at the same time it is our answer to it.

We should continually return to the grace of the sacrament of Baptism, so that through our faithfulness to these extraordinary and particular graces, we may achieve to some degree, a state of purity of our soul such as was given to us in the moment of Baptismal initiation. By the immersion into the death and resurrection of Jesus, we achieve, through Baptism, a certain state of immaculateness, which we often waste later. The graces of Baptism are given to us for a lifetime. We however, often squander them by submitting to evil. If, however, we desire to progress towards sanctity, then through various stages of purification we can once again reach this particular state of immaculateness, which we had wasted through being unfaithful to the graces of Baptism. Our whole path to sanctity is nothing other than achieving the same state of our soul that we received at the moment of Baptism.

Progress in our interior life depends on an ever stronger desire to actualise the graces of Baptism, graces of being moulded to the image of Christ by living in the spirit of the eight Beatitudes: "[...] Whoever loses his life for my sake will find it" said Christ (*Mt* 16:25). This "losing of one's life" begins with the sacrament of Baptism and is to be actualised throughout our whole life. We should lose our life for the sake of Christ by trying to imitate Him ever more fully on the path of our life according to His will and His plan for us. We have to be 'buried' with Christ. Because of this, we must go through our own death. That is why, as far as we have not died to everything that separates us from God, our holiness, our life: "hidden with Christ in God" (comp. *Col* 3:3) cannot become a reality. By losing our life for Christ, we respond to the call to find ourselves in Him who is: "the whole fullness" (*Col* 2:9).

The "gift of faith" (GE 2) given to us in the Sacrament of Baptism, should lead us to the steady growth of our adherence to Christ. Baptism stands before us not only as something accomplished, but also as a certain mission and purpose. Similar to faith, Baptism is a mission for us that will not completely be fulfilled until the moment of our union with Christ, when we will be able to repeat the words of St Paul: "Yet I live, no longer I, but Christ lives in me" (*Gal* 2:20).

Incorporation into the Church as the Body of Christ

An important redemptive consequence of Baptism is the *incorporation of the newly baptised into the community of the Church*. The faith that is born in Baptism, causes us to come out of the seclusion of one's 'self', and allows us to enter into communion with Jesus as well as with those who are part of His Mystical Body. The Church becomes the place of our faith. Our faith becomes a part of the Church's faith. If we were separated from the Church, our faith would have no chance of development.

According to the statements of the Vatican Council II, the Mystical Body of Christ is built by Christian sacraments of initiation. Through Baptism, we are incorporated into it, and subsequently we are strengthened by Confirmation and the Eucharist. However, the perception of our belonging to the Mystical Body of Jesus and our gaining life from this belonging, is impossible without living faith.

Very often the people present at a baptism are as if blinded; they look, but they do not see or understand. Unaware that an event is taking place which is beyond our imagination, they are more interested in the child's behaviour – if it is crying or remains quiet. If they had faith, they would be shocked because they would realise what great an event is taking place at that moment when the water is poured on the head of the person being baptised, and the words: "I baptise you in the name of the Father, and of the Son, and of the Holy Spirit" are said. Only living faith allows you to see past the simple sacramental signs to the inconceivable reality taking place at that time. Lack of faith may either lead one to comprehend somewhat magically the causality of the sacrament of Baptism, or it may lead one to comprehend it as a purely external function of the Church.

One cannot build or deepen one's personal faith, of which Baptism is the source, only through private dialogue with Jesus, because *faith is also communion with others*. Also in this dimension faith is to be born and developed. The sacrament of Baptism is a very important event for the entire parish. Prayers, together with the attitude of faith provided by the nearest community of the faithful, should accompany the person receiving this first sacrament of the Church. It is through this sacrament that God grants special graces not only to the newly baptised, but also to the community accepting him. This community receives a new, sanctified member. It is important then, that we should all accept this great gift of God in the spirit of deep faith and gratitude.

Through the Sacrament of Baptism, one enters the communion of saints. The grace of Christ, like a powerful ray of life, penetrates all who belong to His Mystical Body. The same Holy Spirit acts in everybody. One receives

His graces not only for yourself, but also for others; spreading these graces through word, thought and works of love. Growth in grace, through a greater faithfulness to God, intensifies one's specific influence on others like invisible radiation. This influence is brought about not only through the spoken or written word, or by giving a good example but also regardless of our direct actions or physical distance. As Romano Guardini has said, the prayers of others belong also to you, just as their actions, their spiritual growth, and the purity of heart. Have you ever reflected on the community of the suffering, on the fact that the graces flowing from somebody's suffering are transferred to others? *If united with the suffering of Christ, you offer your painful experiences to God for others, then your experiences become a living, beneficial redemptive power for them.* Beyond all obstacles and distances, you bring help where nothing else can be of help (see R. Guardini, *Il senso della Chiesa*).

No one is a lonely island. As the Mystical Body of Christ, we constitute a specific network system, similar to a system of connected vessels. Your every good as well as evil, has its social dimension because it brings out a specific supernatural basic pressure for good or evil in others. Prayer, seen in the light of faith, situates itself within the system of connected vessels. In such a system, it is never a solitary prayer. As a member of the mystical organism of the Church, you either enrich or impoverish it through your prayer of faith. This determines the ecclesiastical dimension of prayer and defines your responsibility towards the Church and towards others. We are not talking about thoughtless saying of prayers, but of authentic prayer, which as a form of realisation of faith, reaches God Himself. In order to have an effect on others, prayer does not have to have the character of a clear intercession for someone. It is enough that faith, hope and charity grow in you at the same time as your prayer life intensifies, the Church and the whole Mystical Body of Jesus, will be able to feel the beneficial, saving influence of your prayer.

Within the Mystical Body of Christ understood in this way, there are mutual bonds of varying degrees of closeness and depth. The physical image of *a system of connected vessels* can enlighten for us the mystery of mutual bonds within the Mystical Body of Christ. A family, as a domestic church, can be an example of a system of connected vessels. Usually God, wanting to affect a particular group of people, uses one of them in a special way so that through him or her, He can bestow the others with graces. Let us assume, for example, that in a certain system of connected vessels as a family of four, three people are closed to life in grace. They are like hermetically sealed test tubes. If just one of the persons tries to turn towards God, he or she becomes a channel of grace for the remaining persons that are close to him. This person has two possibilities for influencing the others. He can try to remove the stopper from above, just as a corkscrew removes a cork. But if the stopper is made up of live tissue of human personality, then forcing the access from the top will always bring about suffering, painful and destructive wounds, as well as significant limitation of personal freedom. God does not want all this. He loves His children to make decisions in *freedom* of choice aiming for fuller faith and love. Continuing further with the image of connected vessels and sealed test tubes – one can say that God prefers that stoppers be pushed out from below, by the specific pressure of grace within your test tube. Before converting others, try first of all to be converted yourself. The greatness of your faith and your adherence to Christ, is important: "It is not important what you do", said John Paul II: "it is important who you are". *The more good there will be in you and the more faithfully you will follow grace, the more effective your influence on others will be.*

Therefore, if a wife wants to convert her husband, who, for example, has a drinking problem, she must begin with her own conversion. It is she who must first be converted. Her spouse may be converted through the basic pressure of goodness increasing within her. This can only be brought about when she grows in grace and deepens her conversion. The reformation of the world and the transformation of others must begin with ourselves. The life of Christ must first increase in you to such an extent, that the graces and good accepted by you cause the conversion of others. It may happen that this kind of conversion will remain ineffective; that it will require an ever greater 'pressure' of grace in your 'test tube'. This is when God may ask you to lead a more intense spiritual life, and even to offer yourself completely to Him, which amounts to a radical striving for sanctity. These are the consequences of your belonging to the Mystical Body of Christ, consequences of this extraordinary truth, that through Baptism, you have become a member of the Total Christ, of His Mystical Body.

G. K. Chesterton writes that throughout the history of the Church, the Christian faith suffered a seeming death at least five times (see *The Everlasting Man*, 250-254). One of these dramatic periods: "when the Church was dying", was during the time of St Francis of Assisi. Among documents which give testimony to a very dismal image of the Church in the XII century are numerous papal bulls (edicts) written by Pope Innocent III condemning scandals of usury, venality, gluttony, drunkenness and debauchery. Along with the fall of morality a lot of fanatical and aggressive heresies arose in Europe which nearly destroyed Christianity. Another blow to the Church were the wandering preachers who continually criticised the clergy as being often preoccupied with the greed for wealth. They preached that the clergy were the opposite of the model of Evangelical poverty.

Francis never criticised anybody. He believed that if evil is all around, it is he and not others who must first be converted. If such great abundance of wealth and debauchery is rife, then it is through his fault. It is he who must become radically poor and pure. Saints differ from those who create heresies because heretics want to convert others but do not want to convert themselves, whereas *saints turn all the cutting edges of criticism towards themselves, they strive to be converted so that the world can be better*.

The more rot and scandals St Francis saw around him, the more he desired to conform to the image of Christ in pureness, humility, and poverty. It was he, Francis, whose fault it was that the world was so evil; therefore, it was he, Francis, who had to be radically converted and history proved that he was right. For when Francis was converted, when he became so 'transparent' to the Lord that the image of Christ could be reflected in him, Europe then began to heave itself up from its fall. The dream of Pope Innocent III came true. He dreamed that a figure resembling Francis was supporting the unsteady walls of the Basilica of St John in Lateran, named the:"mother and head of all churches" (which is a symbol of the whole Church) and he saved it.

By the power of Francis' sanctity, Christ raised His Church from the 'death' of faith. The world was enriched by his sanctity, not so much in the way of learning about a man who actualised the spirit of the Gospel in an extraordinary and heroic way, but in the way of the system of connected vessels, as his sanctity affected people that he had never come into contact with. The light of faith lets you see that through Baptism, you belong to the Body of Christ, that you were included into the system of connected vessels of this Body. This Body so greatly needs the converted and the saints. It is in great need of your conversion and your sanctity. Thanks to the light of faith, you come to know that the reformation of others should always begin with yourself.

Every one of your good deeds affects others. *Your faithfulness is the strength for those that you love.* When you receive Holy Communion, not only are you strengthened but also your spouse, children, brother, friends, parish, the Church and the world. Begin then with yourself, with your own opening up to Christ. God wants you to be sanctified and through this, He wants to sanctify your environment, your loved ones, the Church and the world.

Priesthood of the Faithful

The common baptismal priesthood of the faithful is most fully expressed in the offering of the Eucharist. Not only does the priest celebrating Holy Mass represent Christ-The Priest, but also the faithful. Together with the priest, and through his intercession, they offer the sacrifice of Christ, and offer also themselves to God. Vatican Council II speaks of this expressly: In Baptism, to the faithful Christ "gives a share in his priestly office, to offer spiritual worship" (*LG* 34, compare *LG* 31), to "offer the divine victim to God and themselves along with it" (*LG* 11). "The baptised, by regeneration and the anointing of the Holy Spirit, are consecrated to be a spiritual house and a holy priesthood, that through all the works of Christian men and women they may offer spiritual sacrifices" (*LG* 10). In the sacrament of the Eucharist the baptised resemble Jesus Christ in a special way, for not only do they collaborate in the offertory, but they themselves also become the offertory gift.

The common priesthood of the faithful is connected with the call to offer everything to God, with the call to holiness. Your Mass, celebrated within the common priesthood of the faithful, is good when you actually offer yourself to Christ completely, and through Him fully offer yourself to the Father; when you want nothing for yourself and accept being denuded similar to Christ. *God, who is jealous of your love, desires this total gift.* The priesthood of the faithful should lead you towards a greater engrafting of yourself into Christ. You must, like Christ, be a total gift to the Father, reserving nothing for yourself, for only then will He be able to offer Himself fully to you and fill you with Himself.

The increasing presence of Christ in you should be passed on to others. Through Baptism you have been called to *contemplata aliis tradere*, to pass on to others that by which you live. Through Baptism you become a member of the prophetic office of Christ. *You are therefore called to per-*

form apostolic and evangelisational functions.
St Peter connects the priesthood of the faithful with the
duty of the apostolate and of evangelisation: You are in the
'royal priesthood', you should announce everywhere your
love of Him, who called us out of the darkness into His wonderful light (comp. 1Pet 2:9).

The Holy Father, in his homily given on 29th January
1979 in Mexico, said: "All the faithful, by the power of the
Sacrament of Baptism and Confirmation, are obliged to
publicly profess their faith. A faith which they have received
from God, through the Church. They should spread it and
defend it like true witnesses of Christ because they are called
to evangelization, which is a fundamental duty of all members of the People of God". However, you must remember
that the efficacy of your apostolic efforts will flow from
a deep interior life. It will flow from a life of prayer and
total devotion to Christ-The Priest by following the example of Mary, whose virginal and total devotion to God became the source of her spiritual motherhood for souls. Baptism, through which you are born into faith, also calls you
to such motherhood.

Chapter 2

Confirmation

The Sacrament of Confirmation is closely related to Baptism and to the Eucharist, because it is also a sacrament of Christian initiation. If baptism incorporates the baptised into the Church, then Confirmation performs a further, more perfect incorporation into the Body of Christ. The Sacrament of Confirmation multiplies the dynamism of the graces originating in Baptism and endows us with a special strength of the Holy Spirit. Hence, by the sacrament of Confirmation we are more strictly obliged to be witnesses of Christ, to spread and defend the faith (see *LG* 11). For people with faith, Confirmation along with Baptism and the Eucharist is a requirement for the process of being transformed to the image of Christ, to take place and deepen.

In the Sacrament of Confirmation, we receive the grace of Pentecost, the full outpouring of the Holy Spirit. In liturgical texts, the Church compares the graces of this sacrament to those extraordinary graces, which were granted to the Apostles on the day of Pentecost. Confirmation is the solemn 'descent' by the Holy Spirit into the baptised. The Holy Spirit desires to bring that which was begun once and forever in Baptism, to maturity. A special fruit of this sacrament is the *gift of mature faith* given to us by the Holy Spirit.

Fullness of Faith Requires Denudation

Our faith deepens while we are being stripped of our own systems of security, of all that begets feelings of strength, power and importance in us. The stripping of us makes room for faith and demands our humility. By stripping us of our power and strength, God brings us closer to Him, places us in the truth and causes us to need Him more. This is an extraordinary grace.

St John of the Cross has said that *God loves a soul most, when He strips it*, for one can then achieve *the fullness of faith*. When you have no support in any of your systems of security, then God can attract you to rely solely on Him, the only rock of your salvation. *The grace of denudation is a special gift of the Holy Spirit, who before descending onto a person, strips him*. Often we do not understand fully the work of the Holy Spirit. We know that He is the Power, the Paraclete and the Love of the Father and the Son; but we often forget that it is *He who is the principal Author of our holiness*. Therefore, He is the One who brings about the entire process, which is indispensable to us on our path toward unity with God. This process has elements of attraction and elements of purgation. It is the Holy Spirit who denudes us; it is *He who renders us to become poor*. He is the one who endows the poor, since He is called: "the Father of the poor", as professed in the Hymn of Pentecost.

Does the Holy Spirit endow us in order to make us rich? This would make no sense since according to the Gospel, being rich in spirit is a curse. *Stripping us* and making us even poorer *is His gift* so that we may be more open to His strength and to His love. Only then will *He Himself, become a gift for us*, for then he will be able to descend into the emptiness of our nakedness and fill us with His infinite power and love.

A particularly important kind of denudation, through which the Holy Spirit prepares us for His 'descent', is the process of stripping us of the false image we have of ourselves and freeing us from living in falsehood. In the Gospel, St John relates the promise of Christ to us that the Paraclete – the Holy Spirit, will convince the world about sin when He comes (acc. *Jn* 16:8). This is one of the functions of the Holy Spirit, who descends upon us in Confirmation, is to convince us of our sin, therefore *bestowing upon us the grace of humility*. This is a fundamental grace of the Holy Spirit. It is because of this grace that we come to know who we really are, and we become convinced that we are sinners and people of little faith.

If you are self-confident, if until now you have not yet discovered your own sinfulness and are self sufficient in everything, then in reality you do not need the Holy Spirit. The attitude of self-confidence and the lack of humility close your heart to His descent upon you. If you do not feel yourself a sinner, you will not desire the redeeming action of the Holy Spirit in your life and then you will not receive the graces of the sacrament of Confirmation. *Humility and faith*, these fundamental gifts of the Holy Spirit, *open us ever more fully both to His descent upon us and to accept the Holy Spirit Himself as a gift*.

The Fruitfulness
of the Sacrament of Confirmation

The graces of a sacrament do not work automatically. Confirmation does not erase the faults in your character, does not eliminate inadequacies in your temperament, and will not substitute for your own efforts. After its reception, you could still remain miserable, fearful and lukewarm in your faith and a slave to the consideration of what other people think about you. The strength given to you by the Holy Spirit in the sacrament of Confirmation is initially only proposed to you, so that you may freely accept it through faith. You can reject this grace and disregard it. The Holy Spirit comes to a person very gently, without imposing Himself, in the silence of the heart that is hungry for His coming. He will come only when you are hungry for Him, when you yearn to hear every word of His and desire His work within your life. The Holy Spirit will come to you, depending on the extent of your hunger for His presence and your yearning for His works in your heart.

The path towards maturity of faith is not a regular movement in a straight line. It is usually marked with many ups and downs. In order to reach the maturity of faith, you must often experience faults of your own immaturity. First you must become humble; then you can grow in faith. The growth in humility, which is truth, will enable you to open yourself all the more to the graces of Confirmation and grow in them.

After receiving Confirmation you may consider that you have completed a certain stage in your religious life, while in reality, it is the beginning of your journey towards fullness in the life of faith. It is a sacrament that requires your co-operation. Confirmation initiated something extraordinarily important in your life. It initiated a new process of your co-operation with the Holy Spirit, who has come to you and is waiting. He is waiting, that through the growth of your humility and faith, your heart will be completely opened for His descent upon you.

Before receiving the Sacrament of Confirmation, during the renewal of the baptismal profession of faith, the Church asked you a question: "Do you believe in the Holy Spirit, Lord and Giver of Life, whom you are to receive today in the sacrament of Confirmation just as the Apostles received Him on the day of the Pentecost?" In order to answer this question once again, you must stand in the truth before God. When looking at your life in the spirit of humility, which is remaining in the truth, should you not question your faith? How little faith there must be in you if you do not live by the graces of Baptism and by the graces of Confirmation. What has changed in your life, since you accepted the fullness of the Holy Spirit? If you were baptised as a baby, you were unaware of the great transformation, which baptism brought about in you and you were unaware that this was your rebirth. It was then that your parents and Godparents professed the faith on your behalf. Later, during Confirmation, you renewed this profession of faith... Were you fully aware at that time, that you were choosing Christ, that you want to belong to Him completely? Trying to remain in the truth, often pose the following questions to yourself: What did I do with the gifts of the Holy Spirit? What have I done with the Holy Spirit Himself, whom I received as an inexpressible gift?

The validity of the sacrament does not imply its fruitfulness in the person who receives it. A sacrament may be valid, but in spite of this, one may not receive the graces connected with it, or even worse, one may be guilty of unworthy acceptance of the sacrament. St Paul, speaking about the Eucharist, warns: "Therefore whoever eats the bread or drinks the cup of the Lord unworthily will have to answer for the body and blood of the Lord" (*1 Cor* 11:27). The sacraments bestow grace only upon those who do not resist it. The Holy Spirit needs your openness, your internal disposition. He stands at the door and knocks, but He will not enter uninvited. You can, therefore, close yourself to Him or you can, through faith and humility, open the doors of your heart wide to Him.

The Sacrament of Confirmation received in a state of mortal sin or without faith is valid but nevertheless dormant and fruitless. However, it can begin to awaken when you are properly disposed. The Holy Spirit descended upon you in the sacrament of Confirmation. If you had received this sacrament with little faith, not realising the importance of this extraordinary event, then you can repair this now by becoming increasingly disposed towards it. The graces of this sacrament should revive and grow in you through your whole life, until you achieve full unity with Jesus in the Holy Spirit.

The Gift of the Holy Spirit to the Apostles

During the Last Supper, Jesus said to the Apostles: "I have much more to tell you, but you cannot bear it now. But when he comes, the Spirit of Truth, will guide you to all truth" (*Jn* 16:12-13). On the day before Christ died, the Apostles were still unable to accept all of His teachings, as the Holy Spirit had not yet descended on them. Why did the Holy Spirit not descend upon them immediately at the beginning, when they first met Jesus and followed Him? If this had happened, they would have then fully understood His teachings, whereas up to now they understood little of what Jesus told them. The Holy Spirit, however, could not descend upon the apostles at the beginning because they did not possess the necessary disposition. They were not yet denuded, they did not have true humility and they also lacked an authentic faith. A faith, which would enable them to remain helpless and to await everything from God.

A person of faith must be stripped from his systems of securities. This was very apparent in the lives of the Apostles. The process of denudation leads either to rebellion and to turning away from God, or to greater dynamism of faith and to a more trustful self-entrusting to God. The rich young man, who with much fervour asked Jesus what he should do to achieve eternal life, ultimately refused to follow the Lord. He did not want to leave everything – That is why, referring to him, Christ said: "It is easier for a camel to pass through the eye of a needle than for one who is rich to enter the kingdom of God" (*Mk* 10:25). The apostles were astonished and Peter's reaction was: Lord, what will happen to us who "[...] have given up everything and followed you" (*Mk* 10:28).

A certain feeling of superiority and satisfaction could have arisen in Peter's soul. He could have said: "That man did not follow the Lord, but we really did leave everything." No one can contradict this. Peter really did leave his family and his profession, just as John and James did. We know from the Gospel, that they left their father Zebedee, who most likely had some kind of fishing business, because he employed hired workers, and was probably a rich man. They, like Peter, left their families, professions and safeguards; they left everything in order to follow Jesus. However, usually a person is ready to give up everything for God in one go, but then, just as easily, he is ready to claim everything for himself, once again.

The Apostles, for example John and James, had given up everything for Jesus and later became so very self-confident. They had a clear vision of a temporal kingdom of Israel and wanted to make a career for themselves in this kingdom. Moreover, it seems that they were jealous of Peter because he was set apart from the others. Their mother, surely not without their knowledge, asked Jesus that they be seated on His right and left side. Thus, one can give up everything only to reclaim everything later. In their desires, these Apostles had claimed pre-eminent positions in the kingdom of Jesus for themselves. They really are true Pharisees in their spirit, even though they are not Pharisees formally or nominally. In order to see clearly their Pharisaism, let us recall the situation when Jesus, on His journey to Jerusalem, wanted to pass through a Samaritan city. The inhabitants of this city would not accept Him, due to their intolerance towards Jews. It was then that James and John, called the "sons of thunder", said: "Lord, do you want us to call down fire from heaven to consume them?" (*Lk* 9:54). This is a true characteristic of Pharisaism; that they, regarding themselves as more superior, demand to punish those, who in their perception, are inferior.

You may leave everything, follow the Lord and then regard yourself greater and more superior than others, and by doing this, you are accepting the poison of Pharisaism. This also happened to the Apostles. We see, however, that as long as they were so very pharisaical, as long as they claimed so much for themselves, the Holy Spirit could not descend upon them. Surely it would have been the easiest way for the Holy Spirit, the Paraclete, to descend upon them in the very beginning and explain all the teachings of Jesus. He is the One who sanctifies and makes straight the paths in human souls, and He is the light. However, *the Holy Spirit will not descend into a person rich in spirit*, as Jesus said: "But woe to you who are rich" (*Lk* 6:24). He cannot descend into a self-confident person, who is rich in spirit, because this kind of person is not open to the strength of the Holy Spirit who is the *Father of the poor*.

In the lives of the Apostles, various *stages of their coming closer to God* can be clearly distinguished. At first, there was a Galilean spring in their lives, joyous and full of dreams. It was not until later that dark clouds begin to appear on the horizon. Conflicts with the Pharisees arose and this gave rise to fear and dread of them. These were the first signs of purgation and the first trials of faith in their lives. Thomas, a witness of the attempts to stone and arrest Jesus, with resignation and close to despair, said: "Let us also go to die with him" (*Jn* 11:16). Then, they were no longer the triumphant Apostles in their Galilean spring. They started to fear because they were getting closer to a confrontation with the elite of the nation, with the power which in those times was wielded by the Pharisees and the Sadducees.

A supreme purification and a genuine trial of faith occurred during the Passion of Christ. Good Friday, the day of Jesus' Passion through which the Redemption of the world was brought about, was a night full of purification for the Apostles. Then, everything fell apart for them; everything collapsed. There was no kingdom; Jesus was defeated; there was no perspective for future; there was nothing to wait for and only despair remained. John must have also felt this despair when standing at the foot of the Cross, although the Gospel does not mention this directly. He must have been totally crushed.

Some may say: If you have not gone through a trial of despair, then you really do not know anything. The Apostles went through this kind of trial of despair on Good Friday. Being Pharisees in spirit, the Apostles were then stripped of everything. After the Resurrection, the appearances of the resurrected Christ enlightened that night of purgation. They saw that He was alive and that He was present among them. However, this was a new presence, a presence that did not give a feeling of complete security or stability. It was connected with the newly risen humanity of Christ. This humanity is different from the former one; it is glorious and can no longer be confined to earth. His risen body can pass through closed doors, so sometimes the Apostles doubt whether it is really their Master that they are seeing.

The trial of the Apostles, their night of purgation, was not yet completed. The ten days between the Ascension and the Pentecost brought with them trials of faith and further denudation. Their main support, the humanity of Jesus, was then definitely taken away from them (compare R. Garrigou-Lagrange, *Les trois âges de la vie intérieure*, vol. II, p. 352, 420). Then, they had nothing to rely on. *The young Church being born in the 'upper room' and devoting Herself with one accord to prayer was stripped of everything.*

The second night of purgation, the night of the spirit, was the most difficult one. The theology of spiritual life states that it is then when one encounters Mary, who through her presence illuminates this night. And this is what happened after the Ascension in the 'upper room'. The Apostles were not alone there. Mary, who never succumbed to despair and whose faith never faltered, was with them. She was among them as an example of faith and perseverance in prayer, an example of looking for the Holy Spirit to come. The Apostles being truly poor, owning nothing, unable to see the humanity of Jesus, waited together with Mary. This was when the Holy Spirit, the Father of the poor, as is stated in the liturgy, came down upon the Apostles who had been stripped of everything and left in complete emptiness. Then the strength of the Holy Spirit descended upon them. Only once they were strengthened in this very way, were they sent to conquer the world for Christ.

To Love the Church

Through Confirmation, you are even more closely bonded to the Church. By receiving this sacrament, you enter into a very close spiritual bond with the bishop who performs this rite. The Bishop as a minister of the Sacrament of Confirmation, partakes in the supernatural motherhood of the Church. By becoming a special channel of graces and of gifts of the Holy Spirit, the Bishop 'gives birth' to the fullness of Christian life in you. The liturgical texts talk about a spiritual stigma that is imprinted on the soul of the confirmed person, expressing a close and perfect bond with Christ and with the Church. When entering into a spiritual bond with the bishop, a confirmed person is called to love the Church. You should love the Church as much as Christ, who "handed himself over for Her" (*Eph* 5:25). This means loving Her to the point of giving one's life for the beloved Church.

The Church is our Mother. Because of widespread secularisation, our perception is that the Church is far from being supernatural. In the Apostle's Creed we profess: "I believe in [...] the holy Catholic Church". This profession corresponds to an attitude expressed like this: I devote myself trustfully to the Church as if I was to devote myself to the Person of Christ.

By your entrusting yourself to the Church, you entrust yourself to Christ. Abandoning yourself to the Church, you abandon yourself to Christ, because the Church is His Mystical Body.

Henri Daniel-Rops in his book titled *"Nocturnes"* writes about a mosaic from the 4th century AD, in a Bardo museum in Tunis. No Christian can look at that mosaic without being emotionally moved. It imperfectly portrays a front porch and colonnade of a basilica. It is made of antique stones resembling graffiti. Beneath, there is a small inscription that causes this mosaic to become an expressive symbol. The inscription consists of two significant words: *Ecclesia Mater* – Mother Church.

The 4th century was a time of great wars, of paganism, which was returning time and time again, and of persecution by Julian the Apostate. It was not easy or safe to openly admit that one belonged to Christ. Throughout the empire there was increasing unrest, political anarchy and religious turmoil. Among continual threats and danger, when the blood of martyrs was still fresh in amphitheatres, someone wrote two striking and consoling words surely engraved in the atmosphere of comforting prayer. Mother Church.

Does it require much imagination, Daniel-Rops continues, to understand those words in the same way our distant brother in Christ understood them, when He arranged them with small stones into damp cement? The world that surrounded him was uncertain and the fate of the world remained shrouded in darkness. And yet, there existed a place where even danger made sense, and a great hope dominated everything. It was a place where human brotherhood overcame class and race divisions, where love was stronger than death. The basilica columns and walls were only a symbol of this privileged place. An Apostle said that it will be the house of the Living God forever. This place is the Church, our Mother, *Ecclesia Mater*. Many centuries and epochs passed, and the Church still remains the same for us, as She was for the faithful in that heroic century, she remains our Mother.

If the Church is the Mother, then a Christian may call himself a son of the Church. However, the word 'son' expresses a relationship other than membership in human associations and parties and other than that found in various philosophies and philosophical systems. Is the name Father ('papa' = father = 'pope') given by us to the one we consider to symbolise and personify the Church, not an echo of this very bond and of complete trust which the African inscription 'Mother Church' conveys? The role of the Church becomes particularly visible during times of threat and unrest. It was said that the Church was dying and that along with the remnants of the past She was relegated to the junk heap. However, She still stands in Her place, like a city set on a hill visible to all. When in times of threat we call for help, our Mother the Church is invariably there. Being boundlessly patient and merciful, She always welcomes the prodigal son with joy, opening Her arms to every lost sheep.

The Church believes that no betrayal is so great that it cannot be forgiven. Therefore, the Church looks with indescribable compassion upon those who have been rejecting Her for years, and softly whispers: *Does it really matter that you have wandered so far away from me? I have always been near you.*

The Church today, from the very depths of Her maternal heart, offers the same support to the people of the 20th century as She did to the people of the 4th century. In the face of great historical storms, in a world tormented so often by barbarianism, where people have lost understanding of the sense of human life, in the world doubting everything including itself, the Church alone gives the impression that She knows well, what She is aiming for. The Church alone reveals unchanging truths, despite attempts to accuse Her of striving for significance in public or political life.

In a world possessed by violence, concludes Henri Daniel-Rops, in which man seems to be fascinated with the tragic fatality of his own death wish and the prospect of total destruction, the Church repeats a simple, and much needed lesson of love. She Herself received this lesson on the hillsides of Galilee and the Blood of God sealed its truth on Calvary. In repeating this lesson of love, the Church remains *Ecclesia Mater.*

Through Confirmation, you were very closely bonded to the Church. Being enriched by the graces of Confirmation, did you come to love Her as Christ loved Her? Are you interested in Her life, do you call Her "my Church"?

Your desire to be united with Jesus will cause you to feel even more that you are a son of the Church. Seeking Jesus, you will find Him fully in His Mystical Body; by loving Him, you will begin to love the Church, which He loved to the very end, to the point of giving up His life.

Apostolic Responsibility

Love of Christ that deepens through faith, begets the desire to be a witness of Christ. *Your call to sanctity and your love for the Church are also closely connected with the call to apostleship.* Reminding Christians of their obligation to witness for Christ, John Paul II says: "Only profound love for the Church can support the fervour in giving witness. Faithfulness to Christ cannot be separated from faithfulness to the Church".

The Council stresses that Christians "inserted as they are in the Mystical Body of Christ by Baptism and strengthened by the power of the Holy Spirit in Confirmation are assigned by the Lord Himself to the apostolate. [...] The apostolate is lived in faith, hope and charity poured out by the Holy Spirit into the hearts of all the members of the Church. And the precept of charity, which is the Lord's greatest commandment, urges all Christians to work for the glory of God through the coming of his kingdom and for the communication of eternal life to all men" (*AA* 3). Therefore, everything that you do should serve to build and expand the kingdom of God.

You have received a treasure and extraordinary gift, which you cannot keep solely for yourself. This would be burying the treasure. You are to pass on this priceless treasure and share it with others. You should witness about that which has been bestowed on you, what you have found, about what you love and what the Holy Spirit has brought about in you. The more you surrender to the Holy Spirit, the more He will be able to form the image of Christ in you. The Holy Spirit, having deepened the love for the Church in your heart, will cause you to be faithful to your call to the apostolate.

John Paul II once asked France: "Are you faithful to the grace of your Baptism?" This question is also directed to you: Are you faithful to the grace of Holy Baptism? Are you faithful to the graces of Confirmation? Are you growing in your sense of responsibility for the image and life of your Church, diocese and parish?

The rite of Confirmation refers to concrete forms of witnessing about Christ, which should always flow from faith and love. You are to give witness to the One who died for you and was resurrected. He also died and was resurrected for those to whom you give witness about Him. Your apostleship should be an attitude of service to others strengthened by the Holy Spirit. You should also pray to the Holy Spirit for the grace of fortitude, which is so necessary to defend faith and to undertake the difficulties of apostleship.

Confirmation will remain a sacrament unknown to you if you do not come to know the Holy Spirit. It will be a sacrament unknown to you if you do not realise that He continuously purifies and renews you. He is forming in you a filial attitude to God the Father and is praying in you, in the words of a child: "Abba, Father!" If you realise this, then He will be bestowing on you the peace of Christ, not as the world can give. Above all, He will draw your heart to the poor so that you will strive to help them not only materially, but also spiritually, by proclaiming the Good News of salvation and love of God, which you will experience for ever more.

During his first pilgrimage to his homeland, on the eve of the Feast of the Pentecost, John Paul II called out:

"Let Your Spirit descend!
Let Your Spirit descend!
And renew the face of the earth.
This earth!"

You will not see the Holy Spirit with your physical eyes, but He exists. Only through faith can you see and accept His redeeming actions. If you do not have faith, if you do not try to listen to Him, or if you actually drown out or stifle his usually quiet voice, then you: "grieve the Holy Spirit"

(*Eph* 4:30). An attitude such as this if adopted by you would be the source of His torment, the source of His abasement through His contact with you. He, who is the Spirit of Jesus sent to you, who is the Love of the Father and Son, continually reminds you of the words of Jesus, speaking sometimes with the force of a windstorm but most often with the gentleness of a tiny whispering breeze. It is so easy to drown out His voice and through your own fault waste this extraordinary gift that is bestowed upon you in the Sacrament of Confirmation.

Faith, which is a necessary condition for the work of the Holy Spirit in the soul of the confirmed, is an authentic encounter of two persons. The Holy Spirit desires to continuously deepen this encounter and through this, to lead the soul to greater unity with Christ and to contemplation and sanctity in the service of the *beloved* Church.

The Eucharist

A close interdependence exists between our faith and the sacraments. Vatican Council II in the "Constitution on the Sacred Liturgy", emphasises that the sacraments not only presuppose the presence of faith in those who receive them, but they also nourish faith, strengthen it and express it (cf. *No.* 59). Faith is always the preliminary condition for the efficacy of sacraments, as the strength of sacraments correlates with the strength of faith. Dogmatic theology states that although the sacraments impart grace by themselves, *ex opere operato*, they remain fruitless if faith is lacking.

Because of little faith, many Christians do not involve themselves in the redeeming work of Christ's death and resurrection, which can be brought to full realisation through the sacraments. Those Christians, in spite of frequent reception of the sacraments, do not develop spiritually.

Looking for the Redeeming Action of Christ to come in the Eucharist

Perhaps you are wondering why the Eucharist and the Sacrament of Penance are not transforming you; they do not seem to bring visible results. You are not transformed because grace needs your openness and internal disposition. Look how the Church, in her wisdom, endeavours to prepare for the special graces of Christmas throughout the liturgical year. She dedicates entire weeks in Advent, praying incessantly for the coming of Jesus, for His coming down to earth: "Let justice descend, O heavens, like dew from above" (*Is* 45:8), she entreats in her liturgical prayers. The Church desires that hunger for Jesus and for His coming, continue to grow within us. The graces of Christmas dwell in our hearts, to the extent of our hunger and desire for His coming. His rebirth will come within our hearts at Christmas, to the extent of our preparation and our openness, therefore to the extent of our faith. If there is no Advent, then Christmas is not adequately experienced. If you do not experience the message of Advent and therefore do not look for Jesus to come, then do not be surprised that Christmas seems to slip by without leaving a mark on your soul.

As we look for the coming of Jesus during Advent, we should also look for the coming of Jesus in the Eucharist. Jesus continually descends onto the altar, is born for us and His birth on the altar should also be preceded by an 'advent' – a Eucharistic advent.

Eucharistic advent is above all an attitude of faith. It is faith in the love of Jesus who awaits you as a loved one. It is so important for you to believe that Jesus desires to come into your heart, that He desires the celebration of the Eucharist. He waits for you to receive Holy Communion, because He wants to give Himself to you fully through The Most Blessed Sacrament, the main source of graces.

One of the most fundamental psychological needs in a person is the need for acceptance and love. However, do not look for acceptance and love in people through whom you will often experience disappointment and embitterment. Faith tells you that in reality you need only one acceptance, the acceptance from Christ, who always accepts you. John Paul II said: In Holy Communion, you do not receive Him as much as He receives you, He accepts you as you are. He receives, which means He accepts and loves.

At about 178 AD, the pagan syncretic philosopher Celsus wrote a dissertation full of hate and sarcasm in which he mocks the Holy Mass and derides Christian dogma regarding the Incarnation and Redemption. According to Celsus, the Christian faith is a sheer madness because Christians believe that their God became one among them and that they can be united with Him through a sacred banquet. This is, in his opinion, simply madness. This opinion of

Celsus should be reversed. It is God's love for man, which is the folly and not the Christian's belief that Christ offers Himself in the form of bread. The Eucharist is an expression of Christ's folly. His folly is His love for man, and His love for you, which is beyond human prudence and foresight. You should prepare yourself for the coming of Christ in the Eucharist by believing in the folly of His love. St Francis de Sales strove to prepare himself for the coming of Christ in the Eucharist all day, so that if asked what he was doing, he could have answered that he was preparing for the Eucharistic Sacrifice.

It is so important that your faith in His love increases and that you believe ever more firmly in His ardent desire to come to you in the Eucharist. When you finally come to believe in how greatly He loves you and awaits you, then you will realise that if you delay, *God experiences in His folly love for you that, which psychology calls the torment of looking for someone to come*. When you start to believe that Jesus loves you, that in fact He waits for you, as a consequence of your faith the hunger for God, the desire for the Eucharist, should awaken within you a painful yearning for His coming. The torment of looking for a loved one to come is similar to the torment of love that is rejected. The more a mother loves a child who is not returning, the greater is her torment in looking forward to seeing him again. Even more so, if it is the infinite love of God, which you cannot even imagine. How great then must His torment be in looking for you to come?

Belief in His desire to meet with you will prevent you from falling into routine behaviour, which is one of the greatest threats to your faith. When you come to believe fully in the infinite love of Jesus and when you realise His torment of looking for you to come to the Eucharistic Table, *then you will no longer be able to live without the Eucharist*. Your hunger for God and your burning desire to meet the Lord will be within you, and routine cannot co-exist with that hunger.

The Eucharist as the Culmination of Faith

The sacrifice of Christ, according to St Thomas Aquinas, is fruitful only in those who are united in faith and love with the passion of Christ. The greater your faith and love, the more effective the Eucharist will become in your life. Faith is sharing in the life of God and becomes actualised in a special way through the sacraments, all of which are sacraments of faith. *Through the Eucharist, you join the community of believers as they celebrate Christ's death and resurrection*; you become jointly immersed in this unfathomable mystery: "The liturgy unites us all in the explicit celebration of our faith, especially during the Eucharist. At no other time is the faith of the Church so complete. At no other time is the Church so much aware of Her union with Christ who died and was resurrected, and aware that the Church looks for Him to come again. At no other time do we share in the faith of our community, as at that moment when we pray together, when we make our offering together and together we unite with God's love which is in Jesus Christ" (J. Colomb, *Le devenir de la foi*, ch. 4).

In the Eucharist, Jesus immerses us in the mystery of His death, and then our conversion and transformation is being brought about; then the death of our 'old selves' occurs. A resurrection and rebirth will occur also within us through the strength of sacramental action and the redeeming passion of Jesus. Our immersion in the death and resurrection of Jesus causes 'new selves', conforming to the image of Jesus Himself, to begin to be born in us.

As the Eucharist is the adherence to the person of Christ, then accepting Christ and clinging to Him is fully expressed only when we partake in the Eucharist, which is the culmination of faith. During the Eucharist, Christ becomes the gift offered to the Father for our sake. Through the common royal priesthood, we also are called to give a complete offering of ourselves to God in union with Christ who offers

Himself to the Father. Our adherence to Him means communion with His gift. It means giving our lives to God in order for them to be transformed and to become a service to the Church and to our brothers. The purpose of the Eucharist is your conversion, your turning away from your own will so that it may gradually disappear in your service to others. You go to Holy Communion to be converted, to establish the reign of Christ in your heart from now on and for His will to become your supreme value. *Every reception of the Eucharist should confirm your adherence to His will*. Consequently, you should wish that Jesus will foil your plans. The Eucharist should prepare you for this; it should contribute to the gradual demise of your egoism, allowing Christ to grow within you.

As faith is the reliance on Christ and entrusting yourself to Him, then in the Eucharist you should entrust to Him all of your affairs, fears and anxieties. The Eucharist will then bring you peace born of the faith in the redeeming power of Jesus' sacrifice. This faith means believing that He redeemed you from fear, uncertainty and stress, and from all that destroys your spiritual life, as well as your physical or mental health. Through faith you will be able to receive the fruits of Redemption.

Faith is the acknowledgement of your own helplessness and sinfulness and the awaiting of everything from God. Therefore the Eucharist as a *par excellence* sacrament of faith, *calls you to have the attitude of a helpless child and sinner*, who longs for nothing more than being healed of his own evil. During Mass, make every effort to stand before Jesus like the leper in the Gospel and pray that Jesus will cleanse you from the leprosy of egoism, from the leprosy of your pride, the leprosy of your concern for yourself, of your hurriedness, unrest and sadness. Then, ask Him to take away your leprosy of being excessively concerned about temporal goods, because all these things make the growth of Christ within you impossible.

During Mass, faith will enable you to come to know yourself, your sinfulness and your need of Redemption. You will begin to see yourself in truth more fully, to the extent of deepening your faith. You will perceive the leprosy of your sin, and then you will come to know how unworthy you are of the Eucharist, and simultaneously, how very much you need its saving action in your life.

Your growth in faith will enable you to discover *the real presence of Jesus and to discover the making present of His redemptive sacrifice.* You will begin to know Him even better, who He is and what happens on the altar. Try to participate in the Mass as if it were for the first or for the last time in your life, so that receiving the Eucharist every day does not become a routine for you that destroys your faith. Reflect on how intensely a priest must experience his first Mass after ordination. Certainly, when he takes into his hands the Body of Christ for the first time, he becomes aware of the real presence of Somebody. His hands might even tremble at that moment, for he has faith untarnished by routine. Imagine the first Holy Communion of a convert, who after preparation for, and after receiving the sacrament of Baptism, receives the Eucharist. He may receive the Body of Christ with trembling lips, for so strong and alive is his faith that it is God Himself, who is present on his lips, and that it is God Himself who enters his heart. He may believe that he finds himself in the face of an unfathomable tremendous mystery, full of majesty – *misterium tremendum.*

Kenosis of Christ

Faith allows you to see that *your hands and lips that receive Jesus are always unclean* – even when you are in a state of sanctifying grace because you are always a sinner, and the hands and lips of a sinner always remain unworthy and therefore unclean. "How very unworthy I feel I am, of this grace of the altar, which I used to approach so boldly" Cardinal S. Wyszyński wrote in his prison notes

(*Zapiski więzienne*, 7th April 1955). Just think, you receive Jesus with your lips that can kill with words. Your words sometimes wound and are the source of harm and unhappiness, instead of uttering blessings. And yet these sinful lips come into contact with the highest sanctity of God. If you consider all this you will come to know the mystery which theology calls 'kenosis' (from the Greek *kenosis* – a complete humiliation).

The Eucharist is a kenosis, that is, the Self-humiliation of true God and true Man, as Jesus in His greatest sanctity comes into contact with your sinfulness and your unworthiness. This does not mean, however that you should avoid the Eucharist, for when you receive the Eucharist, It makes you more worthy of receiving It again. Jesus waits for you with His love, He wants to come in order to transform you, to sanctify you, and to make you increasingly more worthy of His coming.

St John, the Apostle, said: "If we say, 'We are without sin', we deceive ourselves and the truth is not in us" (*1 Jn* 1:8). We are all sinners and we are all unworthy to receive Jesus. Think about your lips as being unclean, but you should also expect that the Eucharist will remove that uncleanliness, that leprosy of sin, that leprosy of egoism from your lips and from your heart and soul. Jesus desires this so very much that He wants all this to be done even at the price of His great humiliation, at the price of His kenosis. It is in the light of faith that you will see how greatly the Eucharist is the Self-humiliation of Christ. He strips Himself of His divine dignity and humiliates Himself by the very fact that His majesty and His humanity are hidden in the material form of bread and wine. He strips Himself from His due praise and honour. When you come to him with your sinful hand, with sinful lips and a sinful heart, this is a further kenosis for Him.

St Louis Marie Grignon de Montfort advises us to invite Mary to participate in the Eucharist with us. *The presence of the Immaculate Mary close to us*, especially during the Eucharist, *is a great mystery for us, and it is a solution to the problem of the kenosis of Christ*. Those who find it difficult to acknowledge the need and importance of the Marian way to Christ, are convinced that Mary cannot stand between themselves and Christ, for she would overshadow Jesus. However, in the light of faith, in the light of the knowledge of God's holiness, in the knowledge of your own great unworthiness and your sinfulness, you will find that situation is not the case.

When you are asking Mary to stand between you and Christ, you become closer to Him, because *when you ask her to stand between you and Christ, you do it so that she may spare Him kenosis*, His Self-humiliation. Only her hands are clean and were never unclean; they were and always will be immaculate. Here are the only human hands and the only human lips which are clean and immaculate, which are worthy to touch the Body of Christ. When you strive to lessen the Self-humiliation of Christ by asking Mary to receive Him for you and through you, then you give praise to the kenosis of True God and True Man. You link the attitude of humility, an attitude of acknowledgement that you are a sinner, with the faith in His incredible love for you. This love, at the price of the self-humiliation that is beyond your imagination, wants to bestow upon you the fruits of the Redemption.

Chapter 4

Listening Intently to the Word of God

A close interdependency exists between faith and the Word of God as well as between faith and the sacraments. Reading the Holy Bible requires faith, as well as active cooperation and conversion. The realisation of the Word of God is required in everyday life, which should be a life flowing from faith. Faith is the response to the Word of God; it is listening intently to the Word in order to live it every day.

Encountering the Word of God

We can regard the Biblical text in two ways: *impersonally, as an object* – when it is seen as an object which we examine, or as an aid to find the solution of a problem which interests us; or *personally, as a subject* – when the text we read becomes for us a 'mystery', as understood by Gabriel Marcel. If you read the Holy Scriptures with the intention to broaden your religious knowledge, that means that you regard it as an object. The Bible treated as an object, is simply 'a thing'. This relation toward the Holy Scriptures is necessary; however, it is insufficient.

Certainly, the Word of God for the Church is the principle source from which we gain knowledge of God; thus it should sometimes be regarded as an object. Nevertheless, the Holy Scripture is also an inspired text and a source of revelation, therefore *our relation to the revealed text, should primarily be a personal one*. In fact, the Bible is not 'a thing' but above all, 'Somebody'. Christ is most fully present with us in the Eucharist, but in another way He is also present and alive in the Bible. When reading the Holy Scriptures, you encounter a living and true Christ through the gift of *faith*, which He Himself gives to you. The Church states that the Eucharistic table has a double meaning. It is the table of the Word of God where the faithful receive, through *faith*, the revealed Word of God. It is also the table of the Body of the Lord, where the faithful are nourished with the Body and Blood of the Lord when celebrating the 'sacrament of faith'. Therefore it is right to say that one should approach the Bible in the same way as one would approach the table of the Lord. That is why, when you take the Bible into your hands, you should do this with respect, veneration and profound faith. This should be done with a different gesture than reaching for any other religious book, since this is a Book filled with God's presence.

The Presence of God in the Word

Every person affects the environment by his presence; this does not occur with things. Only when we meet a person do we encounter the presence of someone and through this we enter into either a desired or inconvenient realm of their influence. The Holy Bible is 'Somebody'; it is the presence of God. Therefore, when taking it into your hands, you enter into the realm of that very Presence. It becomes a 'mystery' for you, a truth that grasps you and into which you are immersed.

You will find your Lord in the Bible, and that is why your contact with the revealed text has a special meaning. *It is contact with God, who loves you and who desires to affect you with His grace*. This contact leads you to inner conversion – and that is its greatest purpose. You should therefore read the Bible not to satisfy your curiosity, nor to gain knowledge or to find a solution to a problem that is nagging you – although this will be needed at times. You should take advantage of this form of contact with the Lord in the hope that He will bestow you with the grace of conversion. *If you enter into a person-to-person relationship with Christ who is present throughout the inspired text, this text will permeate you*. Then you will begin to *listen intently to the Word of God*, understand better the thoughts and desires of Jesus and begin to know Him even better: 'Ignorance of the Holy Scriptures is ignorance of Christ', warns St Jerome. Listening intently to the Word of God will influence your choices and decisions. You will want them to be in accordance with His teachings and His desires. *The reading of the Holy Scriptures is a fundamental factor of your growth in faith and of your sharing in God's life*. It is the looking at oneself and the surrounding realities as though it were through the eyes of God. God reveals Himself to us through the intercession of the Word, leading us through knowledge of God towards love. He reveals himself so that by believing in His Word we may adhere to Him and entrust ourselves to Him. If you attempt in faith to share in the thoughts and desires of Jesus, then they will eventually become your thoughts and desires. If you remain in the realm of His presence, the genuine Presence, then you will become like Him in the same way that you become like the people you associate with – "Like father like son". By listening to the Word of God and taking in its essence, you will begin to empathise with Christ in His experiences in the Gospel and in what He is, at present experiencing. *Your intense contact with Christ, who is present in the Word of God, will cause you to identify with Him even more.*

Every word recorded in the New Testament and every gesture of Jesus is an expression of this mystery of the Presence. You should allow it to overwhelm you; you should learn to listen intently to it. This unimaginable Presence requires your particular openness that will in time cause your total transfiguration *for you to become, as if transformed into Christ*. The purpose of your life will then be achieved, that is for Christ to increase within you and reach His fullness.

The Role of the Word of God in Prayer

The presence of Christ in the Word of God will overwhelm your interior life and your prayer. Listening intently to the Word of God will cause you to meditate on words, which shall be engraved deeply into your heart. They will later come to mind during moments of prayer, which will then become prayers based on the Bible, and also they will come to mind in moments of making decisions. Have you already asked yourself, what role does the Bible play in your prayers?

Christ often used a specific literary form, the parable, which is an expanded symbol that draws your attention and engages you. Because of this, when you read, for example, the parable of the Good Shepherd, you can truly recognize yourself among the sheep led by the shepherd. You can also imagine yourself as the lost sheep loved by Christ the Good Shepherd, Who never stops searching for it. And when He finds it He sets it on His shoulders with great joy. The symbolism of the parables of Christ draws you into the realm of His works. *In such a simple and accessible way, He teaches you to love and to believe in love*. If it has happened that you have fallen greatly and your soul is shrouded in darkness, then maybe you will recall the parable of the Prodigal Son, which will let you believe once again that He has never stopped loving you. The parable will teach you the attitude of the repentant son who with amazement and gratefulness welcomes the joy of the forgiving father. Similarly, when some storms occur in your life you may be reminded of the storm on the Sea of Galilee. Then you will realise that just as Jesus slept in the storm-tossed boat of the Apostles, He also 'sleeps' now in the boat of your heart. Nevertheless He is present within you, and when He is there, nothing bad can happen to you. All this may help you to include the Word of God into your prayers, which will allow you to regain an inner peace.

Through your reading the Bible, a true image of God will be formed in you. You will avoid distorting His image, which so often occurs. Maybe you are afraid of Him, or maybe you do not believe enough in His love because your love is little. Your love should continue to grow until you die. *Prayerful meditation of the Bible will teach you about the love of God, who loves you incessantly, because He is love.*

Meeting with Christ who is present in the Word of God will also help you to discover God in the world around you. It will teach you to interpret the many symbols through which you can discover His presence in nature and even in the phenomena of civilisation and culture. Sheep, for example, reminded St John Vianney of the love of the Good Shepherd. The sight of sheep deepened in him the awareness of the great love Jesus had for him as a shepherd of a parish. Moreover it reminded him of Jesus the Good Shepherd's love for those whom He entrusted into St John's love and care in order for Saint John to be their shepherd. The sound of a mountain stream reminded St John Vianney of the words in the Gospel about the 'living water' welling up to eternal life (cf. *Jn* 4:14; 7:37-39).

Someone once said of himself, that he enjoys watching the lights on the streets and in houses and the lights of passing cars at night. It reminded him vividly of the fragments in the Bible and especially in the Gospel according to St John, which states that Jesus is the light of the world. Every light, therefore, became a symbol of Christ for him, bringing to mind, "the true light, which enlightens everyone" (*Jn* 1:9).

If you want your prayers to be also based on the Bible, you have to be like Mary from Bethany. In Bethany, with his friends Mary, Martha and Lazarus, Jesus found a place of shelter and rest for Himself. When the final days of His life were approaching, He, knowing that the Pharisees were spying on Him, went into hiding in Bethany. Earlier though, when Jesus came to their home, Mary sat at His feet and listened intently to every word spoken by Him; she behaved as if she were before a tabernacle. When a busy Martha asked Jesus to speak to her sister that she was letting Martha to do all the serving, He answered her: "Mary has chosen the better part and it will not be taken from her" (*Lk* 10:42). *This better part is to be beside Christ, to sit at His feet and listen intently with faith to His words spoken to us through the Bible.*

Mary, listening and contemplating Jesus,the Word Incarnate, must have been His great joy. Whereas we, being so often busy and anxious about many things, feel that we do not have the time to read the Bible. For Mary, however, there was nothing more important than the fact that He, the Master, was there in her home. The most appropriate place she found for herself was at His feet.

Following the thought of Jean Guitton (*La Vierge Marie*), the Blessed Virgin Mary should be called the Virgin of Meditation (*Virgo Meditans*). Her Hymn, the *Magnificat*, is a testimony of how much the Bible was a source of life for Mary. It is a testimony of prayer based on the Word of the Lord. The Bible was her 'nourishment' and source of prayer.

For thirty years, Mary absorbed the Divine presence of her Son. *That is why her face portrayed the Face of Jesus in the most perfect way,* and this is the source of her greatness. How important it must have been to Christ to create this Masterpiece, *His most perfect image*, since He devoted Himself to Mary for as much as thirty years. She continuously absorbed His thoughts, His desires and His will, thus becoming more and more unified with her Son.

You encounter the presence of Jesus in the pages of the Bible. You should, therefore, just as Mary did, absorb His thoughts and desires in order to live by them later. You should imitate Mary completely and to the end, in becoming open to the great work of Christ who transforms us into His image.

The Bible should be for you a place to encounter Christ, who has loved you to the end. He desires to form His Image also in you, just as He did in His beloved Mother.

Chapter 5

Prayer as an Actualisation of Faith

Prayer and faith are not separate realities that are merely mutually dependent or exist side by side. Prayer is always closely connected with the reality of faith; it is the meeting of a person with God in faith, and finally it is a form of actualisation of faith. If faith is adhering to Christ and entrusting oneself to Him, then, prayer is the giving of oneself in complete devotion to Christ, to be accepted and transformed by Him in a new way. If faith is the acknowledgement of one's own helplessness, and the awaiting of everything from God, then prayer is the existential calling of spiritual poverty and inner emptiness of a person, so that the Holy Spirit may fill him with His presence and strength. As one's faith develops, prayer becomes purer and more ardent. Prayer, as an actualisation of faith, is marked by the dynamism of conversion. Similarly, the Eucharist and the Word of the Lord lead a person towards transformation and towards conversion.

The Example of Christ

When we read the words of the Gospel, we quickly discover that the Good News confuses us. The Gospel is so contrary to our natural tendencies that it seems an unceasing paradox. The Gospel overturns our human concepts. Christ Himself did just this.

He was awaited for thousands of years. Everything was orientated towards this unique event in the history of the world, which was to be the coming of the Messiah, the coming of The One who will perform the work of the Redemption. After such a long period of expectation Jesus revealed Himself only to the shepherds and the Wise Men. Then for over thirty years He led a secluded life, far from activity, at least in the sense of the activity which was expected from a Messiah. In the eyes of the world, those years appear to be wasted. For if someone is awaited for thousands of years, he should give the most of himself. Multitudes of people are waiting, and here is Christ, 'wasting' thirty years in Nazareth. When this wasted time, in terms of human activism, was over, Christ showed Himself by the river Jordan and was proclaimed by the Holy Spirit Himself. Then Jesus retreated and went into the desert. Thus, we are yet again confused and cannot understand at all, this attitude of Jesus. We would like to take Him aside and rebuke Him, as Peter the Apostle once did. We would say: "Lord, what on earth are You doing? Multitudes are waiting, and yet You are going off to pray again: Have You not already prayed for so many years?" Yet He, who will later say: "The harvest is abundant but the labourers are few" (*Lk* 10:2), left the harvest and went into the desert to pray incessantly for forty days. Does this not amaze us?

The Evangelist Mark writes: "Rising very early before dawn, he left and went off to a deserted place, where he prayed" (*Mk* 1:35). Pay attention to this detail: "before dawn" which means that it was still night. *Christ, wanting to pray, deprived Himself of His sleep*. Being astonished, we would again want to cry out: "Lord, do you really need this prayer at night at the cost of your health?" Each day in Christ's apostleship was exhausting. Even in the evening, people would come from the whole city or area and bring to Him all who were ill and possessed. It is difficult to say when His everyday work ended. It may have ended at midnight, for the multitudes left Him unwillingly. After such a hard day and exhausting evening, Jesus still deprived Himself of His little sleep.

When we speak of Jesus being besieged continually by multitudes, we have to say that this was closely related to His praying in solitude. There is an especially important message for you, hidden in all of this: in order for your contact with people to be fruitful, *you have to know beforehand how to leave for seclusion*. You have to appreciate a time of desert in your life. How great a role the time of the desert must have played in the lives of saints. Think of how much John the Baptist needed solitude in the desert, and of how decisive was the life of St Ignatius Loyola as a hermit in Manresa, or the role of the hermitage in the life of St Benedict in Subiaco. Modern man, affected by activism, seems to think that he must continuously give more of himself, *but what really is to be given?* One might think that Christ, who was so completely unified with the Father, did not need to pray at all. But He continued to do so regardless of His need to sleep. And it was always like this. Being besieged by people was always the result of withdrawing *to meet with God*. However, if on your part there is no withdrawal to pray and meditate, but only an escape from people into your own personal affairs, then another kind of siege will occur, a siege of your own egoism. This will also be a desert for you, but not a life giving one, as was Christ's or the saint's desert; this will be a desert of destruction and not of life (cf. A. Pronzato, *Ho voglia di pregare*, p.64).

The Priority of Prayer

A fundamental question arises here: how much time do you devote to prayer in your everyday life? What place does prayer have on your list of the most important things you are to do? Before what and after what do you place it? *Does it head the list* of your life's affairs, or is it the least important? What about your day of recollection? What about your examination of conscience, which is the looking at yourself in the face of God? The answers to these questions will indicate *what is more important than God in your life*.

At this point you may begin by objecting, that with the whole mass of duties, it is difficult for you to find the time to pray. Cardinal Lercaro, the Archbishop of Bologna, during a meeting with priests, spoke with his unique fervour and ardour about the necessity of half an hour of meditation every day. After the conference meeting, during the discussion, one of the young priests stood up and said: "Of course, your Eminence, in theory this is clear and simple, one should meditate... but when? My day looks like this: I get up in the morning at 6:30, at 7:00 I say Mass, after that I listen to confessions, then religious instruction, lunch and after lunch I have lessons with the boys in the oratory, then I visit the sick, I work in the parish office, and I have pastoral meetings. In the evening, I work with youth groups until about midnight. Where am I to find time for half an hour of meditation if I can barely find time to say the breviary?" "You're right," said the Cardinal. "you really don't have time for half an hour of meditation. Your activities 'smother' you to such an extent that you have no time to pray. If you can not afford half an hour to meditate, you should meditate not for half an hour but for one and a half hours." (A. Pronzato, *Ho voglia di pregare*, p.113) Of course, this was not intended to be a bright, paradoxical response. The tragedy of our Christian activism is that *activities really do smother us*. This young, zealous priest, who was devoting himself to God and to saving souls, was so smothered by activism that he needed a greater antidote.

If you look at yourself in the light of faith, you will understand that *the more suppressed you are with activities, the more time you should dedicate to prayer*. Otherwise, you will be empty; you will have the impression that you are giving something but this will only be an illusion. *You cannot give that which you do not have*. It could be said to the young priest who was talking with Cardinal Lercaro: What of it, that you devote so much time to your ministerial work, that you spend so much time with the boys in the oratory, that you visit the sick, that you hear confessions and have pastoral meetings, all of this is like trying to carry water in a sieve. The exhausted, overworked, busy priest, trying to carry water in a sieve, does not realise who is the One who really makes all the decisions. To say that this priest has no faith would be too emphatic, but his faith is undoubtedly poor. With his attitude, he seems to say: It is I, who is making history, be it only in my own area, in the parish or some other place; it is I who decide who will be a believer; the salvation of others depends solely on my work. Meanwhile, *everything depends on God*; it is He who decides and only He can give you strength. If He involves you in His work, this does not mean that you are irreplaceable. So many times God has shown us that He can manage very well without us. If you have seen this in your life, then you have received a great grace. God needs us only because He Himself has wanted this. He can save people who have not attended classes in religious education, as we have often witnessed. There are some people who come to church and to confession, who have never attended a single religious lesson and yet the seed sowed by God gave new shoots in their souls. *God* does not need human intervention but despite this, He *wants to involve us in His redeeming works of saving the world*. If, however, we feel that everything depends on us and on our work, then we are trying to carry water in a sieve. When overworked, it is easy to forget that we should first of all, want to have an audience with the One on whom everything depends, who holds the fate of the world and the fate of each one of us in His hands.

In the light of faith, the most important activity in our day is prayer. It must take precedence over all other activities. *Contact with God determines the value and importance of our work*. Its efficacy depends on what is, as it were, in the back room; therefore, it may depend on your knees that may be hurting very much from kneeling.

According to John Paul II, it is not important what you do, it is important who you are. It is important that you are like the Pope, a person of faith and prayer. When a Christian, as a disciple of Christ, stops being a person of prayer, he becomes useless to the world, he becomes like tasteless salt worthy to be: "trampled underfoot" (compare *Mt* 5:13).

The issue of prayer is a major issue in our Christian vocation. By praying, we not only pay homage to Christ on our own behalf, but we worship Him in the name of the whole world, which either does not know how, or is unable to, or does not want to pray. One thing is certain: if we do not pray, no one will need us. The world does not need empty souls and hearts. When we ask, what is the relationship between prayer and action, then the priority of prayer and sacrifice should be emphasised in relation to action. We can bring God into the lives of children whom we catechise at home or in school, only to the extent of our having begged for it earlier on our knees. The issue of the relationship between prayer and action can be summarised in the statement: all authentic action is born of prayer and contemplation. For everything that is great in this world comes from God; everything that is great in this world is born of sacrifice and prayer.

Kinds of Prayer

Prayer is the crucial issue for every Christian. *You are as much a Christian as you are capable of praying*. Prayer, and its particular stages, are signs and indications of your closeness or distance from God. The stages on your path to God are indicated by various stages of prayer. At each one there is a different form and kind of prayer – because prayer is the expression of your bond with God.

There may arise in your life a stage of dryness at prayer, stripped of emotions. It is then difficult to pray. Therefore, we may be tempted to resign with the thought that this prayer is pointless. However, it is then that your prayer may have a special value because you will begin to undertake the effort to pray, all the more only on account of God.

A particularly meaningful story told by one of the saints, is the tale of the King's musician, their mutual love and the drama of the musician. It is a true drama for a musician to lose his hearing, and this is exactly what happened to this Kings musician. He began to lose his hearing and very quickly became stone-deaf. His music stopped giving him pleasure and he went through sheer torment when playing his instruments. Nevertheless, the King still wanted to listen to his music and so the musician carried on playing, but now exclusively for the King.

You feel good when you feel the presence of God while praying. Prayer can then be something appealing and you may be convinced that you are only praying to God. However you will discover the fuller truth about your prayer when, like the musician who lost his hearing, you become 'deaf' in your contact with God. You will then be convinced that when praying because of God, you were also to a certain extent praying because of... yourself and that your prayer was not fully free from self-interest nor pure.

Once you start experiencing a state of dryness in prayer, do not give in to the temptation of resignation because it is then, when you feel nothing, that you are praying solely for the King.

We must continuously learn to pray. It is a task, which stands before us at all times. The actual form of our prayer cannot be sufficient for us. We should continuously advance and develop it. When we speak of prayer, *praying in words* most often comes to mind. In this form of prayer, we should emphasise the important value of ejaculatory prayers in which we humiliate ourselves before God expressing our gratitude or asking for the grace of holiness. While praying in words, we must remember that we should pray for that which God expects from us. It cannot be prayer drowned in words. Jesus clearly warns us that we should not pray as pagans who "think they will be heard because of their many words" (*Mt* 6:7).

Faith has a decisive influence on *what you pray for* and on the *intensity* of your prayer. If faith changes our mentality and tells us to put God in first place, then to the extent of its growth, our prayer will be increasingly simplified. It will become more and more subordinate to the work of the Holy Spirit (cf. *Rom* 8:26-27) and ever more concerned with matters of the Kingdom: "But seek first the kingdom of God and his righteousness, and all these things will be given you besides" (*Mt* 6:33). The word "first" is of the utmost importance here. It means for you to put God in first place. Do not resign from your own pace of effort, but *leave all concern for yourself and for the results of your actions to the One whose will is to bestow you with boundless love*. Then, in your prayer, you will fulfil the call of Jesus addressed at St Catherine of Sienna: *"You think of me, and I will think of you"*.

Besides praying in words, which can take the form of a prayer of supplication, a prayer of gratitude or a prayer of adoration, a simpler method exists for our contact with God. *God wants us to continually simplify our way of praying*. If we are to pray without ceasing, according to the Bible, then our prayer must all the time be simplified, as we will not be able to pray in a difficult way for very long. There will come a time in our spiritual life when it will be easier to think about God than to talk to Him. We will then move on to *simple prayers of thought focused on God*, which could be called *memory of the presence of God*. This is a simpler form of prayer than praying in words. It requires a lot less effort. You only have to think of Jesus and realise, that the One who loves you is close to you. Similarly, in the preceding hours when you are preparing to receive the Eucharist; it is sufficient that you turn your will and love-filled thought toward It. Prayer of thought can be an expression of *faith*, which means to strive to think with the thoughts of Jesus or Mary. This should be a thought full of serenity and joy. And the "reason for our joy" is Mary. Hence, our optimistic way of thinking, in the supernatural sense, is like sharing in the thoughts of Mary herself. The prayer of thought is a simple one, though it requires attention and care, so that it may occur as frequently as possible in our lives. Therefore, try to remember and think about the fact that Jesus loves you, that He loves those whom you love and those whom you care about. This kind of prayer of faith will bring you inner peace.

God may desire to simplify our prayer even further. He may want us to become completely silent. Just as we can pray with words or thoughts, we can also pray with *silence*. However, not everyone approves of this form of prayer. Many have doubts whether or not this is a waste of time, because during this time nothing is happening. However, remaining in silence is quite an advanced form of prayer, whether it is before the Most Blessed Sacrament or in the presence of Our Lady. Charles de Foucauld wrote, that "to pray is to look at Jesus loving Him". This form of prayer may take on a form called *prayer of simplicity*, or *prayer of simple regard*. If you have to entertain some people with words, while being with them, then this indicates that they are more or less strangers to you. With a person who is close to you, you can be silent and you will not feel uncomfortable. It is this silence, so expressive in its simplicity, that is the criteria of closeness between two people. Jesus wants us to be able to calm ourselves before Him, so that we simply look at Him and are close to Him without unnecessary words.

It may happen that the prayer of silence also becomes too difficult for us. Then yet another form of prayer may arise, that is *the prayer of gesture. You can pray*, for example, *with a smile*, even if this seems odd to us at first. God really does want our contact with Him to be very simple, He wants it to be the contact of a child with its Father, the contact of a child with its Mother. If you love someone, you can say so much to them with a smile, you can make excellent contact with that person. Why then should we not smile at God or Mary? This is the prayer of gesture. A smile is a symbolic gesture through which we express our closeness, gratitude, love and joy to someone. It is a symbolic form containing many connotations, so that a smile can mean something else each time one smiles. Thus, you do not have to exert yourself to express everything in words. God knows that you are smiling at Him and He knows why you are doing so. Your smile towards God and your joy flowing from faith is a genuine, *par excellence* prayer.

St Thérèse of Lisieux shows us another moving attitude of the symbolic prayer of gesture. About two weeks before her death, when she was gravely ill, she was given a beautiful rose from the convent courtyard. She started plucking the petals and covered her crucifix with them with great piety and love. Then, with each petal, she wiped the wounds of the nailed hands and feet of Jesus. With this symbolic gesture, as she stated, she wanted to relieve the pain of the Crucified Lord, dry His tears (see *The Yellow Notebook*, September 14th, 1897). "Another time," relates Celine: "when I saw her delicately touching the crown of thorns and nails of Jesus with her fingertips, I asked' 'What are you doing?' Then, seeing that this surprised me, she answered with an air of astonishment, 'I am taking out the nails and removing His crown of thorns." (*Conseils et souvenirs*, p.88). A gesture of this kind cannot be replaced with anything. This prayer expressed her desire to relieve the crucified Jesus of His pain. It was an expression of the particular love for the One, who was the Spouse of her soul, and was crucified by sins.

St Leopold Mandič of Padua, a great confessor of our times who spent many hours in the confessional, prayed with the ***gesture of showing empty hands***. When hearing confessions, he held his hands in his lap, as if in this way wanting to tell Jesus: "You see Lord, I am not capable of helping the one who is kneeling before me. I am able to give him nothing. Fill these hands with your grace". If he had wanted to continually repeat this to Jesus, he would have been exhausted, besides, while listening to confessions, it would not have been possible. You can also pray, in various situations, with this attitude of being poor in spirit. You can hold your hands in such a way, being aware that this is always a gesture of petition for Jesus to fill your empty hands with His graces and to make you an instrument of His works.

Prayer of the Poor in Spirit

A close bond exists between faith and prayer, as well as between humility and prayer. Someone said: you learn to pray best in moments when you cannot pray. This is the very opposite of what we would imagine. When it is difficult for you to pray, when you are not successful in your prayers, then, from God, you receive an exceptional opportunity for learning how to pray. *The secret of prayer is being hungry for God*. This hunger for God in us comes from a much deeper level than from feelings or speech. A person whose memory and imagination is tormented by a multitude of useless and even evil thoughts or images, can sometimes, under the pressure exerted by them, pray much better in his troubled heart than the one who has untarnished thoughts and who is able to offer easy acts of love. In our hearts, these experiences give rise to *the prayer of faith of the poor in spirit*. In prayer, we should be humble and helpless. If we will be unable to pray, then the Holy Spirit Himself will descend into our humble soul and will pray in us with such beseeching, that cannot be expressed in words (cf. *Rom* 8:26).

You can experience many difficulties in prayer, but remember, it is these difficulties that cause your prayer to be a prayer of the poor in spirit. You should be grateful, therefore, that you experience difficulties. These difficulties can be of various kinds: they can be, for example, the result of fatigue. St Thérèse of the Child Jesus writes: "I should be worried that I have been sleeping (for the last 7 years) during my prayer and my thanksgiving, but I am not worried!... I think that little children please their parents just as much when they sleep as when they are awake [...]. The Lord sees our weakness. He realises that we are only dust" (*Manuscrits autobiographiques*). Therefore, fatigue can become that 'material' out of which the Lord will shape in you the prayer of a humble man, poor in spirit.

Maybe you will be able to take advantage of other situations that will cause your prayer to become a prayer of the poor in spirit.

If prayer comes easily for you, this is also a gift from God that should not be scorned. However, it is *the struggle to get through to God*, which *brings about the true progress of your prayer*. This struggle is an expression of hunger for God, which constitutes the essence of prayer. The progress of your prayer is brought about *through the desire to enter the realm of God, opening yourself to Him and allowing the Holy Spirit, to pray within you*. This desire itself is most essential in prayer. Are then the results of your prayer so very important? It is important that you desire, that you really want to pray. The greater the hunger of God in you, the better. Through prayer, therefore, you should struggle to get through to God and you should come to love this. God will accept all of your desires even though you feel that they are of no great value. He loves humble gifts; He does not want beautiful flowers but prefers simple and plain ones from the meadow because they do not feed our pride.

Someone once said that among all gifts God likes humble gifts the best, gifts that are not something to be proud of. It is this that is needed also in prayer. God accepts every one of your gifts, even though it may not be worth more than a handful of dust. Solely by accepting your gifts, He will make each of them priceless. Your prayer may be just like a handful of dust, but it will become priceless because God, your loving Father, accepts it. He accepts it with the same joy, as a mother accepts a little flower from a small child, since it is the thought that counts.

It may also be, that you will not have anything to offer God in prayer. Then you will give Him your 'nothingness', your complete helplessness. Offer everything to the Lord. Offer yourself to His disposal, such as you are: small, helpless, and poor in spirit. This will be the best prayer, the best because it is in accordance with the first Beatitude. Prayer of the poor in spirit is a prayer of a man who is empty, in the sense of an emptiness that summons the descent of the Lord, the descent of the Holy Spirit. When God sees a soul such as this, stripped of its own strength, then He descends into it with His strength. Blessed are the poor in spirit, blessed are those who pray the prayer of the poor in spirit.

The Rosary of the Virgin Mary

On the Solemnity of Mary, Mother of God, on New Year's Day, in St Peter's Basilica in Rome, John Paul II prayed: "Blessed are you who believed! Blessed are you! The Evangelist speaks of you: 'Mary kept all these things, reflecting on them in her heart.' You are the memory of the Church. The Church learns from you, Mary, that to be a Mother means to be a living memory, that is to say, to keep and reflect on in ones heart, the joyful, glorious, as well as sorrowful matters of the faithful. Mary kept, remembered and meditated in her heart the matters of her Son and of herself as a Mother who is involved in everything relating to Him. She was the memory in the early Church and remained the memory throughout all ages in the history of the Church".

In the words of the Holy Father, Mary is the memory of the Church. In her life there was the Annunciation, the Presentation of her Son at the temple and the finding of the twelve year old Jesus. If the Gospel states that she meditated and kept everything in her heart, that means that *she prayed by means of these events*. Returning continually in her memory to everything that was important in her Son's life and in her own, it was as though as if she prayed her rosary, but without moving from one bead to another. Mary could not forget for instance that first most important event in her life, which was the Annunciation. She lived the joyous events as well as those connected with the passion and Resurrection of her Son. This was her prayer.

If you pray the rosary, you are praying her prayer. Then you are like an image of the Blessed Mother. *You imitate her in this way of keeping and reflecting on the mysteries of the Son and Mother*. She is the memory of the Church, the memory of those events for each of us. Each one of those events is to be alive in us. Meditating on them, you make contact with these mysteries and they become a channel of grace for you. *To love the rosary is to love the Gospel, it is to love Mary also and to love all which she kept and meditated in her heart and which made up her life*.

A Man of Incessant Prayer

An exceptional man of prayer was Guy de Larigaudie. This was a man, it would seem, to whom God had never refused anything; a great traveller (he was the first to travel from France to Indo-China by car), the leader of French youth. He was someone who came to love God with all his heart and therefore was also able to love fully his neighbours and the world. Beneath his photograph, there was a significant note: "Smiling Sainthood". His religious attitude was characterised primarily by *a prayer of affirmation for the world* and by admiration for its beauty. For if one loves God, then one also loves the world. "Everything," he wrote in his notes: "should be loved: an orchid that suddenly blooms in the jungle, a beautiful horse, a gesture of a child, a jest or a smile of a woman. All encountered beauty should be admired; it should be uncovered even though it is wallowing in the mud, and raised up to God." (*Étoile au grand large*). Of course, this does not mean that in his life there were no struggles or sacrifices, that there were no trials of faith and brave decisions, for sainthood cannot be easy: "To feel, deep within oneself, all the filth, debauchery and steaming human instincts and yet, be above all this, not sinking into it, just as you would walk on a dried swamp, allowing yourself to be uplifted by a kind of lightness, which does not allow ones feet to sink in" (ibid).

"She was probably metis. She had splendid shoulders and the animal beauty of those of mixed-blood with thick lips and huge eyes. She was beautiful, wildly beautiful. There was truly only one thing left to do. I didn't do it. I mounted my horse and rode away without looking back, crying out of despair and rage. I trust that on Judgement Day, if I have nothing else to give, I will offer God all of those embraces, which, out of love for Him, I did not want to know" (ibid).

Chastity is possible if it is built on the foundation of prayer: "It is possible, beautiful and enriching if it is supported on a positive base: a living, total love of God, solely capable of satisfying the immense need for love which fills the human heart" (ibid).

Guy de Larigaudie loved dancing, singing and taking risks. He was an excellent swimmer and skier. He took in all the joys, but throughout all of his feelings and experiences, there flowed the constant rhythm of talking to God, brimming over with faith: "The beautiful foreign women could not understand", he said "that even during the most captivating dance music, my heart kept the rhythm of prayer and that prayer was stronger than their charm or attractiveness" (ibid).

In his prayer for beauty he asked: "My God, grant that our sisters these young girls, have bodily harmony, that they smile and dress with good taste. Grant that they be of good health and of transparent souls. Let them have purity and grace in our hard lives. Grant that they be simple and maternal toward us without being dishonest or flirting. Grant that nothing evil slips between us. And that we, boys and girls, be for one another not a source of fault, but of enrichment." "Between Tahiti and Hollywood," he mentions further: "on the coral beaches and the decks of steamships, to the rhythm of the dance, I held in my arms, the most beautiful women in the world. I had no intention of picking any one of these flowers offering themselves or passionately desiring to conquer. However, I judged it to be worthless. My body was aching, but it was for the sole love of God, that I played indifference" (ibid).

Speaking about the Eucharist, he says: "Daily Communion was for me, each morning, a bath in living water, which strengthened and relaxed [...], it was a nourishing meal taken before the next stage of my day, a tender look at me, which gives me courage and confidence. I have passed through the world as if in a garden surrounded by walls. I have led a life of adventure, going from one extreme to another, on five continents [...] yet the garden walls have not fallen down, and I am always imprisoned. But there will come a day when I will be able to sing my song of love and of joy. All the barriers will be broken. I will obtain Infinity" (ibid).

What was the prayer of faith like, of this contemporary saint? "While looking [...] at the most boring film," he wrote:

"it is possible [...] to pray a mechanical prayer in the rhythm of the pictures or the music, praying for the actors, for the producer, or players with minor roles. Also for the audience which is amused or bored, or for the person sitting next to you on your right or left side. Thus, the time which has passed, will not be wasted." (ibid). In prayer, he finds strength in difficult times requiring his great faithfulness to the Lord: "Hard times come," he says, "when a temptation of sin takes hold of the flesh so strongly and irresistibly, that one can only automatically say, barely moving one's lips and hardly believing in it: 'My God, in spite of everything, I love You. Have pity on me'. There are certain nights, when seated at the back of a church and not being able to pray [...] I can only repeat that simple phrase, which I hold on to, as if to a life buoy so as not to sink: 'My God, I love you in spite of everything' (ibid).

"While cutting down weeds with the aid of a hunting-crop, chewing a small blade of grass, and shaving in the morning, you can tirelessly repeat to God that you love Him very much. [...] Singing to yourself about your past life, and dreaming about the future, thus, in this way to speak to your God in song. And speak to Him also while dancing with joy in the sun on the beach or skiing down on the snow. Have God always close to you as a friend in whom you can confide" (ibid).

"I have become so used to the presence of God in me that I always have a prayer deep in my heart which ascends to the lips like a blossom. This barely conscious prayer, does not stop even when drowsing to the gentle rocking of a train or to the hum of a ship's turbine, even in the rapture of the body or soul, even in the bustle of the city or when your mind is tensed in an absorbing task. Somewhere deep within me is infinitely calm and transparent water that cannot be affected either by shadows or by whirlpools on the surface. [...] My whole life was one long quest for God. Everywhere, at any time, in the whole world, I have looked for His trace and His presence. Death will be for me only a wonderful release from the leash" (ibid).

Chapter 6

Love as the Actualisation of Faith

At His Ascension, Christ assured us that He will remain with us for all time, until the end of the world (*Mt* 28:20). He has remained not only in the Church, not only in the Eucharist, which is the making present of His redeeming works, but *He has also remained in our neighbours* with whom He identifies Himself: "whatever you did for one of these least brothers of mine, you did for me" (*Mt* 25:40). Thanks to the presence of our neighbours around us, everyday-life becomes a challenge to our faith, for it is faith that allows us to look at the world as though through the eyes of Christ and to perceive the presence of God hidden in another person.

Faith works: "through love" (*Gal* 5:6) and in love it finds its fullness of life. Faith invites us to enter 'communion' with God and our brothers. God reveals His love (Greek – *agape*) to us, which we accept through faith, so that we may in turn pass it on to others. John Paul II said, that it is in love, that entrusting oneself through faith to God attains its true character and the dimension of a mutual gift.

Agape

Two basic kinds of bonds exist between people and there are two concepts of love that correlate to them. The first ancient concept given to us by Plato, defines love with the word *eros*; the second, which Christianity presents, is love defined in the Greek language by the term *agape*. *Eros* and *agape* are two types of love, which are at the foundation of two different bonds between people. Plato's *eros* is love towards that which one deems worthy of love. This is emotional love. If someone or something suits you, because of a pretty, aesthetic appearance, or if you like being with some-one or owning something, all of this arises solely from your purely natural feelings and this is Plato's *eros*. You love something that gives you pleasure, that which comforts you. This is an egocentric love, as it always *concentrates on you*, on *your* pleasure.

This love, despite its inadequacies and limitations, and in spite of its self-interest and impermanence, should not be condemned nor destroyed. It is connected with the natural order of things originating from God, but was blemished by Original Sin. It should be purified and transformed into a supernatural love, which is essentially connected with life in grace, and according to the Gospel as well as to the thoughts of St Paul, it is the reflection of God's own love. This love is described by the famous words of St Paul in his Letter to the Corinthians: "Love is patient, love is kind. [...] It does not seek its own interests, it is not quick-tempered, it does not brood over injury. [...] It bears all things, believes all things, hopes all things" (*1 Cor* 13:4-7).

This kind of love in the original Greek language is defined by the term *agape*. In the Christian concept, God is *agape*; a love that descends on a person and loves that which is unworthy of love. This is a spontaneous love, which imparts itself only because it is love. *Agape* is a gratuitous love which encompasses a person. It sometimes seems to us that we should win God over, that we should merit His love. But He loves you because you are His child, not because you are worthy. *Agape is love that creates, that loves you not because you are worthy of being loved but so as to make you worthy of it*. *Agape* desires to create an ever-increasing good in you. Someone who has received special graces from God is surprised that they have been bestowed on him. But the *agape* love descends on the unworthy, descends on us all, for we are all unworthy and we all need this creative love which creates good. The anguish for God, who is love, is that He cannot pour out His love fully, that he cannot boundlessly flood the human soul with this love. God is continuously seeking open hearts on which He may pour out His infinite love, without limits.

For every loving mother, her child will always be the most beautiful, even if he were the ugliest, because it is her own child. Is it important how many flaws you have? Maybe you have a multitude of them; maybe they depress you; maybe you cannot stand them any longer.

But God wants to embrace you with His love; He wants to descend upon you, to create love in you *in order to make you, who are sinful and unworthy, a masterpiece of His love.*

The *agape* love, which descends upon you from above, from God, which you accept through faith, cannot be closed within you. Love, as a value, as a good, must be poured out and must be given further. *Agape* is Christ, who lives in you and wants to love others through you and in you. A person gifted with *agape* love, a selfless love, begins to give love. Strictly speaking, it is Christ within him who begins to love others. Agape is not so much an emotional love as a love of the will, which wants to bestow good on others. The bonds it creates between people can last even after death. It is not important who the other person is ugly or pretty, pleasant or unpleasant, full of flaws and sin, or not. What is important, is that the *agape* love wants to love him so that he may become a better person. That *agape* love, which grows within you because of Christ descending into your heart, is often expressed in trivial things, in gestures or looks. It is very important for you to give out this love in the warmth of your look, in the acceptance, in the wonder, and in the continual, friendly welcome of another person.

The Role of Feelings

Agape is not only a love that creates, but it is also a love that forms a communion, a community of people. Contact between people is often a question of feelings. There are three basic kinds of emotional human relations. The first kind could be emotional relations driven by *positive feelings*. If someone is dear to you and appeals to you, you like them and want to be with them. We can experience such positive feelings in relation to God as well as to man. For example, you might feel content with God. Sometimes a person is 'beside himself with joy' when he remains in emotional contact with God for hours, days and even months. Positive feelings may flood the human soul. In the second kind of emotional relations, positive feelings fade and a certain kind of *emotional emptiness* arises, nothing attracts you to a particular person. This may happen either suddenly or be in the form of a certain gradually increasing process. From a psychological point of view, it can then be said that there is a certain emotional disintegration. In the third kind of relation, the most difficult one, *negative feelings* appear. The feeling of dislike may appear towards a person as well as towards matters concerning God. The latter often occurs during periods of purification. Something may 'push you out' of church, you may feel a reluctance toward going to Confession or Holy Communion and you may have difficulties in your contact with God. Similarly, negative feelings may arise toward another person. Suddenly, someone who was your close friend starts to irritate and repulse you.

Human bonds based on *positive feelings* are natural bonds. These kinds of feelings and bonds may arise within every group of people, even among criminals. They can be bonds among colleagues. You can often meet people that are perfectly teamed with each other, in the sense of natural bonds, based on common interest. However, natural positive feelings are by no means lasting. For example, they may occur at the beginning of a marriage and then fade. What happens when they do fade? A crisis, caused by the growing emotional emptiness, which is difficult to endure, arises. In relation to God, this will be a certain kind of dryness: I do not feel anything in my contact with God, nothing draws me either to prayer, or to confession or to the Eucharist. A similar crisis appears because of lack of feelings towards another person, when suddenly nothing draws you to the person who was previously close to you. Then there arises a specific emptiness in relation to friends and acquaintances.

Finally the third, very difficult situation, when there appears an emotional dislike towards matters relating to God or dislike for another person. In this circumstance, sometimes even heroism is needed to overcome oneself. However, it is then, *when a natural bond ceases, breaks down to some degree or is at least reduced, that a chance arises for a supernatural bond to appear or to be deepened.*

It could happen, that in a marriage the couple is well matched, like two pieces of a split brick, which fit perfectly when put together. In the light of faith this is not an ideal situation, because this is only a purely natural harmony of positive feelings. This is not yet Christian love, the *agape* love, which has to be worked at.

It may similarly occur with children in the family. They do not have to be in full harmony, and it is not the point for there to be no problems with them. The point is, that they try to love each other despite their faults and different individual characteristics, and not for them to be teamed in full harmony.

The Crisis of Natural Bonds

Every community of people, whether in marriage, friendship, or in any group, if solely based on natural bonds, does not have much chance of survival. Someday, sooner or later, it either has to break down or attain a higher level of existence. Looking at all of this in the light of faith, it can be said that it is a good thing that these kinds of crises occur in our lives. It is good when suddenly someone becomes less pleasant, less liked by us, because by this we may get an exceptional opportunity. Then the call of Christ to live by the Gospel becomes particularly significant. This also occurs in relation to God during purifications, which are sometimes intense and rapid. Then you may not feel any contact with God, you may find that you do not love Him at all, that something really repels you from Him, and yet in spite of all this, you still try to be faithful to Him. How very precious Confession is then, when you have no desire to go and how very precious the Eucharist is when nothing draws you to it. And yet you go, because you know that it is He, Christ who loves you, who is there, waiting for you. How much more effort you then give; *your gift of self increases to the extent of the lack of natural bonds*. How good it is that crises occur among us, that there are sometimes misunderstandings in marriage, that children can sometimes fight among themselves because they do not get along with each other. These are the cracks, the fissures, which enable the birth or deepening of supernatural bonds and supernatural love. It is this very love, which is the work of Christ, which is everlasting if allowed to develop. Only this kind of love is strong, strong by the power of Christ, by the power of God. A marriage that is strong in God is a marriage that went through this type of disintegration and was able to reintegrate on a higher level. Blessed is each one who has undergone a similar difficult experience with God, who did not betray Him and who remained faithful to Him, because it is then that his love really took root.

In all of this, there is some kind of great hope, especially for those who worry that it is sometimes so hard for them. It is not always easy to get along with another person. Sometimes it seems that he does everything to repulse us from him. But it is then that this person becomes a special grace for us, because he brings with him the call to transcend the natural bond toward a supernatural bond, toward *agape*. From the point of view of faith, people whom we like the least, are the most precious for us, because they present the greatest chance for our attitudes to be polarised, for us to realise that 'to love' is not the same as 'to like'.

To Allow Christ to Love in Us

The distinctiveness of Christian love is christocentricism in both meanings of this word. Firstly, Christ is the most perfect and unique example of love. *You should love as He loves*: "I give you a new commandment: love one another as I have loved you" (*Jn* 13:34). But for you to be able to love as Christ does, then through faith you have to discover His true Image, as shown by the revealed Word. It is not sufficient to learn about Christ in theory. It is only with the growth of faith that love will grow in you, that there will be a growth of the existential bond with the ideal example of love, which is the person of Jesus Christ Himself. Through faith, which allows you to listen intently to the revealed Word and adhere to the person of Christ, you will come to know Him, who is the example of love, and you will desire to love just as He loved, as He loved to the end. Through faith you will start to absorb His thoughts and desires; you will think as He does, desire as He does and love as He does.

Secondly, *Christian love is the love of Christ in us*. He is our Way, our Truth and Life. He is the One that thinks, prays, lives and loves in us with His love. The magnitude of our love is determined by the greatness of our faith, which allows us to share in the life of God. Imitating Christ is not so much following the example of His deeds literally. It is the adherence to Him through faith, so that His will becomes our will; so that His life can always be visible in our lifestyle.

To entrust ourselves to Christ through faith, means to accept His descending love which allows Him to love us so that He Himself can love others in us and through us. Faith allows us to adhere to Christ, to entrust and devote ourselves to Him in such a way that faith becomes one with love and trust. Faith, which permeates the entire Christian existence, contains in itself hope and love as two forms of the realisation of faith.

It is not easy to love someone whom we dislike. That is why we must open ourselves to Christ and feel like helpless children in the face of the crushing waves of negative feelings. We must have the attitude of a child who is helpless when faced with matters relating to God, people, the surroundings and the environment. This is an attitude of trusting faith, believing that Jesus Himself will come and will love in us even those whom we do not like. It is this kind of attitude, that will enable us to come to the *agape* love. Ultimately, when negative feelings increase in us or at least the positive feelings fade, only Christ is able to love in us. Thanks to Him, our will should have a freedom from emotions, or at least it should strive to have this kind of freedom. His presence in us brings us conversion; it liberates us and grants us grace, thus equally granting us freedom. However, this Presence is realised to the extent of humility in us, to the extent that we are little and helpless before God. Only when we are like this, are we able to accept the love of Jesus through faith. Hence, in this way of understanding, the appearance of a difficulty in our relationship with people is a chance to open ourselves to grace, to the love of Jesus. He descends upon us as a Divine *agape* when He sees how helpless we are with our feelings, while at the same time we are looking for everything to come from Him.

Christ, who descends into your heart, wants to love, wants to give Himself to others and desires their good. He wants to love more and more and to desire the greatest good for others, which in the light of faith, means desiring their sanctity. If you love someone, and worry only about his or her material, temporal matters, then you must realise that you actually lack authentic love. It is not sufficient to be concerned about the affairs of a temporal life, about education, health and material wealth. *You can love fully only when you yourself long for sanctity and when you desire to engraft this longing into others.*

You Cannot Love People
if You Do not Love God

The truth that Christ loves another person through you implies that you cannot love a person without loving God. You alone are unable to love. It is Christ who loves in you.

By loving Christ and becoming open to Him, becoming open to the Divine *agape* which descends upon you, you allow Him to love yourself, and to love others through you. Your opening yourself to the descent of Christ, whether it is through the Holy Sacraments, or in prayer, allows you to love others. *You can give Christ to others to the extent that you accept Him and to the extent that you allow Him to encompass you.* To love another person means to impart Christ to him. You cannot impart that which you do not have. The more you love God and accept Him in this love, allowing Him to live and act in you, the more capable you are of loving others.

To love means to give oneself, to impart good to others. However, it is not sufficient to give only material goods. In the light of faith, spiritual goods are more important. If you do not give them to your near ones, then a specific spiritual 'theft', a specific spiritual 'harm' takes place.
– Surely, they have a right to these spiritual goods. Those who surround you have a right for you to become a pure channel of grace for them as you grow in sanctifying grace and in striving toward sanctity. Your growth in sanctity becomes, in the light of faith, the most precious gift for those close to you. You have to question your love, you have to stand in the truth and ask yourself, whether you really love. You are most certainly convinced that you love your child, because not only are you concerned about temporal matters but you also pray for him. But surely the value and efficacy of your prayer depends not on feelings but on the greatness of sanctifying grace, on the greatness of your faith and love of God. If there is no spiritual life in you, if there is a lack of growth in faith and in God's love then, in the spiritual sense, you become a 'thief', to those around you.

A mother who is a 'lukewarm' Christian and has not adhered to Christ through faith, should realise that because she has not come to love Christ, she does not fully love her child. In not receiving Holy Communion, she also deprives her child, who is precious to her, of special graces. Not being aware of it, she is stealing the graces that he would receive thanks to her Holy Communion's. This is because every participation in the Eucharist and in the sacrament of Penance, every time you receive one of the other sacraments, and every one of your prayers, are always the giving of good to others, due to 'the system of connected vessels.' These connected vessels are a system of our tight mutual bonds within the Mystical Body of Christ. You love your husband; son, daughter, parents, those close to you or more distant from you to the extent that you yourself are converted to God, to the extent that you strive for sanctity and to the extent that no longer do you live, but Christ lives in you.

He, who is the only love and only good, desires to love you boundlessly, and is always seeking souls, which He may flood with the boundless ocean of His love. One cannot love man without loving God. In fact, only saints truly love another person; the ones who fully opened themselves to Christ and in whom Christ can fully live and love.

Self-realisation in Christ

Psychology tells us of an ideal 'self' and an actual 'self'. All of us have some idea of who we would want to be, whose image and likeness we would like to bring about in ourselves. These desires are a reflection of the ideal 'self'.

On the other hand, the real 'self' can sometimes be so repulsive that some people are irritated or even maddened by it. This is not the proper attitude. However, this proves that man does not want to be who he really is, that he has his idealised 'self' and that he desires to be different, to be more like the ideal image of himself.

If through faith, you open yourself to Christ, He becomes your "way, your truth and your life" (*Jn* 14:6). He then starts to show you your ideal 'self' and at the same time makes it a reality. Christ alone, will bring about your self-realisation.

In a believer, the image of his ideal 'self' will be perfected together with his growth in spiritual life and with the development of identification with Christ. Coming to know Christ and adhering to Him gives rise to a desire within us to identify ourselves with Him. Christ then becomes our ideal example of a person, our ideal 'self'. Growing in faith and grace causes a clarification of our ideal 'self', because Christ then grants us ever more supernatural light and reveals Himself to us all the more fully.

We are all destined "to conform to the image of his Son" (*Rom* 8:29), thus, only Christ can be our *true* example of an ideal person. As the image of our ideal 'self' becomes more similar to the image of Christ, *we approach the truth*, for it is Christ Himself, who becomes our way and truth. Moreover, He Himself imparts strength to our will so that we can form our real 'selves' following the example of our ideal 'self'.

Each of us brings about his 'self' only when he loves. I can actualise my 'self', thanks to the ones that I love. Such is God's economy and such is my psychological structure. No one of us can 'bring about ourselves' without relating to another person. Without this, we will never fully be in our relation to other people, everything is almost perfect, and then we do not see the need for heroism. Sometimes, however, a person can put us in such a situation, that without heroism, there would only remain that, which contradicts love.

During World War II, people were often in situations that called for heroic love, either you will strike, or you will be beaten up; either you will kill, or you will be killed. These were exceptional circumstances, but also in less dramatic situations, God will call us to love at a great price. We will then be convinced that we are unable to love and it will be easier for us to understand the profound sense of Christ's words: "I am the vine, you are the branches. Whoever remains in me and I in him will bear much fruit, because without me you can do nothing" (*Jn* 15:5) – without Christ *we can do nothing*. It is Christ who is our life. Without Him, we become like the branch cut from the vine, which withers. A person cannot actualise himself without Christ.

Our self-realisation is brought about, to the extent that we open ourselves to Christ, *to the extent that we allow Him to love from within us, that we allow God Himself to live in us*. If you would fully open yourself to Christ, then you could say as St Paul said: "Yet I live, no longer I, but Christ lives in me" (*Gal* 2:20). Christ really does have such an unusual desire: *He wants to love each of us with a suitable love*; He wants everyone on earth to see His face in a different way.

The Church teaches that there is no love without a cross to bear. In order to be able to love another person, my 'self' must be crucified. However, I am not able to accept this without grace. Only grace will make me capable of this. Grace acts in such a way within us that it is Christ Himself, who partakes in our "I want", in our human: "I want to love, I want to choose good". "For God is the one who, for his good purpose, works in you both to desire and to work" (*Phil* 2:13).

Our will, by which we can choose love and goodness, is weak. Human will is too weak to choose that which is difficult, which requires the crossing out of one's own egoism. If someone has not yet experienced this, then it is certain that someday he will be convinced that he really is unable to love, that his egoism is unable to die. It is only through love that every one of us fully becomes a human being.

Love is an act of will; it is our desire to bestow on others, that which is good. We know that each of us may want something, as much as, for example, five, seventy or a hundred per cent. If we have only a 'ten per cent' desire for love to be brought about, then this is not sufficient to form harmony among people, not sufficient for the process of *integration of people* to begin and not sufficient to love as Christ loved. However, my 'I want' can be magnified by the grace of Christ, so that I will start to want to fulfil Christ's commandment: "love one another as I have loved you" (*Jn* 13:34) not at the ten per cent level, but at the seventy per cent level and even higher. This reveals the life of Christ in us.

Perceiving Christ in another person in no way diminishes the value of that person. By loving Christ, I also love this person. It is because of Christ that another person begins to fascinate us and for us he becomes increasingly better and more beautiful. Christ, when entering the realm of a person's will, makes this person desire good all the more. He makes more and more goodness to be present in that person. This is that person's good, because an accepted grace remains the good of a person, even though simultaneously, it is the good of Christ. Christ enters one's life in such a perfect way, that it is *He, who loves another person with my love, and I who love with His love*. There is no separation or alienation here. On the contrary, thanks to Christ being in me, I become my true self – I love and I grow in love.

If Christ becomes my ideal 'self', then my self-realisation is brought about. On the other hand when I sin, when I say 'no' to Christ, I rob myself of my own 'self'. Then I become even less myself. When I sin I close off myself from Christ; I am isolated. If I close myself to Christ, I become sad, depressed and angry. However, I do not want to be such as this, this is not my ideal 'self'. It is Christ who is the ideal 'self', yours, mine, each one of ours. At the same time, it is He who realises our ideal 'self' in each one of us. That is why he assumes so many faces. This wonderful reality confirms the words of Christ: "I am the way and the truth and the life".

Our self-realisation is brought about through our living in the truth and through our responding to the Divine call to love. Without living in the truth, one cannot talk about love in the supernatural sense. This love is the love of Christ Himself in us. And Christ lives within us to the extent that we beckon Him because we see ourselves in truth that is we come to know our weakness. He lives within us to the extent that we want Him to be our life. A person is not capable of doing supernatural good by himself. The Church does not say that human nature is corrupt, nevertheless, we should be aware that we ourselves are not capable of doing supernatural good, that we are incapable of loving. We ourselves are not capable of undertaking this unusually difficult Divine call, especially the call to love our neighbour, which sometimes actually requires heroism. Christ, in His conversation with the rich man, said: "Why do you call me good? No one is good but God alone" (*Mk* 10:18). Everything that is good in us originates in God: "What do you possess that you have not received?" (*1 Cor* 4:7).

We have to continually return to these words, because the self-realisation in Christ is impossible without living in the truth. Christ said about Himself: "For this I was born and for this I came into the world, to testify to the truth" (*Jn* 18,37). **God is particularly sensitive to the truth.** Ascribing human characteristics to God, it could be said that truth is God's 'weak point'. If you are to be conformed to the image of Christ, then there can be no falsehood in you. Christ who identifies with truth, is uncompromising towards falsehood and pride, towards our claiming His work in us, as our own. The greater the Divine graces which we credit to ourselves, the greater is our foolishness. God, in order to save us from this, will have to limit His graces.

Humility is fundament to our self-realisation. Humility is so important, because **God is ready to give everything to a person who credits nothing to himself.** If you live in truth and acknowledge that you can do nothing without Christ, it is as if you are beckoning to Him: Come and live in me. It is only then that Christ comes.

In order not to credit the works of Christ as your own, try to repeat as often as you can: "It is thanks to You, Christ, that I am myself; it is thanks to You that my husband is so appealing; thanks to You, that the people I meet are so good. This will be a sign of your humility. Everything that appeals to me in another person, belongs to Christ, and at the same time it belongs to that person. If we were to suppose, that someone who fascinates us with his supernatural good, is himself so very worthy of admiration, this would be submitting to an illusion. Every one of us will be convinced, someday, of how weak and sinful he is. Meanwhile, it is out of us, out of you, that Christ wants to create a masterpiece, which will amaze others. Then, you will become more and more yourself, and simultaneously, Christ will grow in you.

Every one of the saints brought about the image of Christ in himself in a different way. It is quite extraordinary that we have so many different kinds of saints. In the history of the Church in Poland, St Queen Jadwiga (Hedwig) was almost like an *arbiter elegantiarum* – she had a specific, and not only, aesthetic taste. She fascinated others with her intelligence and her intellectual and spiritual level.

On the other hand we can learn from St Benedict Labres, who died as a pauper and beggar.

We can also learn from St Camille de Lellis, who, as a young man, gambled with cards, was a rogue and led a life that was probably worse than the life of soldiers thrown out of the French Foreign Legion. Once, when he was already an alcoholic, he saw a monk and suddenly a ray of hope appeared in him, "surely even I can be a different person". Later when he lost at cards and was forced to beg, covering his face with a scarf, once again the desire to stop all this was renewed. He then understood, that what he was doing was degrading; that he was not himself, that he was a caricature of a man. He started to dream that he could be a normal man. He decided to be converted. It was then that Christ brought about St Camille's self-realisation. Christ made not only a normal person out of him, but He made a masterpiece and led him to sanctity.

This is how Christ treats us. He does this, because He wants to become **everything** for us, our love, our way, our truth and our life.

9